Why vote Green

Shahrar Ali

biteback ˅˅˅

First published in Great Britain in 2010 by

Biteback Publishing Ltd

Heal House

375 Kennington Lane

London

SE11 5QY

ISBN 978-1-84954-031-5

10 9 8 7 6 5 4 3 2 1

A CIP catalogue record for this book is available from the British Library.

Set in Garamond by SoapBox – www.soapboxcommunications.co.uk

Printed and bound in Great Britain by CPI Cox & Wyman, Reading, RG1 8EX.

Contents

Acknowledgements

Since 2002, I have benefited from many conversations with Green Party members and activists; exemplifying the best in party politics – intelligent and impassioned engagement with the pressing issues of today, and tomorrow. I am indebted to those members who have enriched my understanding of green politics and helped to enliven my commitment to it. In particular, I wish to thank Brian Orr, Jenny Jones, Peter Cranie, Alexandra Freed, Payam Torabi, Khalid Akram, Siân Berry, Martin Francis, Matt Hodgkinson, Darren Johnson, Miranda Dunn, Adrian Oliver, Shasha Khan, Tim Turner, Joseph Healy, Joe Hulm, Penny Kemp, Danny Bates, Pete Murry, Ian Wingrove, Rupert Degas, Romayne Phoenix, Andy Isaac, Juliet Lyle, Johnny Wharton, Dan Viesnik, Susanna Rustin, Lora Rubner; and, for answering a hundred and one midnight phone calls, Noel Lynch. If this book contains any errors, they are my own.

Outside of politics – I was once described by my sister as married to the Green Party! – I thank my family; and Miriam Ricci, Brian Barry, Sylvia Anglade, Dave Savva, Dee Burn, Ania Rosciszewska and Jack Terry. I have enjoyed debate with academics Tim Crane, Barry Smith and Georgia Testa. I thank Biteback for allowing me to make the case for voting Green.

Beauty is truth and truth is beauty. I dedicate this work to Mirjana, who is an inspiration to me more than she realises.

London, January 2010

Radical politics

Why vote Green? This is a question Green Party activists and candidates get asked all the time. Voters are looking increasingly to the Greens because of widespread dissatisfaction with the conventional way of doing politics.

In this book, I let the general reader know what the Green Party stands for and say why there has never been a more important time to vote Green. I begin by identifying our core values – exploring what underpins our outlook – and looking at the Greens' current political representation. I then elaborate our policies in response to current political issues. What follows is not the official Green Party manifesto; it is an account of Green Party politics from a personal standpoint.

I shall draw upon personal political encounters – my own, as well as those of Greens and others – where this will help to illustrate or inform a political position. Often what goes wrong with politics is that politicians become too remote from the people they purport to serve and their decisions do not result in net good, however well intentioned they may be. When a woman confronted Tony Blair during his walkabout of a hospital during the last general election, he had no adequate response to her anger over a relative told to wait for critical care. Blair could not simply refer her to a health service target that had not been met yet; to do so would have been callous.

By the end of the book, you should have a firm idea how Greens would respond to this and other questions, about value and policy. We will examine issues in greater depth than we could do in a piece of election literature. Along the way, we shall ask – and attempt to answer – questions about the value of non-human things; the role of human motivation and rational cooperation; the difficulty of overcoming negative psychological attitudes; and the promotion of ecological commitment of the sort which can transform society. We will explain why, for the Greens, it is so important to revive the public service ethos; to re-establish learning for learning's sake; protect against religious dogmatism in schools; and recognise the boundaries of free speech. We will interrogate the bad assumptions and ignorant decisions (often with fatal consequences) of politicians claiming to act in our name. Greens would instead respect the stipulations of just war theory; avoid incoherent talk or double standards about 'terrorism' and 'evil'; and seek to reframe our human situation today as one of a collective calling. Ours is no ordinary approach to politics; so let us begin.

Value

The Green Party puts environmental sustainability and social justice at the heart of its political agenda – and it does this with *zeal*. In the opening to the Party's Philosophical Basis we say, 'The Green Party isn't just another political party. Green politics is a new and radical kind of politics.' This ambition is informed by a sense that conventional politics has failed to address the pressing issues of the day and that in order to overcome them we must act together with renewed vigour.

The motivation for radical politics comes not as a free-floating ideology, but as a response to the depth, scale and urgency of the problem. Once we collectively understand our situation: the contribution made by humans to the degradation of the environment and extinction of other species, or the impact consumers in the rich West have had, and continue to have, on the impoverishment of producers in the poorer developing countries, our proper response is to want to change things – and to change them radically.

Later in the Philosophical Basis, the Party affirms its commitment to ecological value: 'Each organism is dependent on other species and on the physical world for its survival. Whereas human value judgements normally focus on human needs, value ultimately lies in the well-being of the whole ecosystem.' (PB203)

In its outlook and approach, the Green Party is nothing if not critically aware and engaged. It seeks to promote values in politics. Without values, one is prevented from recognising social or institutional dysfunction for what it is, from speaking out, or caring to do something about it. One only speaks out and acts against injustice because one cares about injustice or harm. Not to care is potentially to fail as a human being, or to fail in one's education, in the broadest sense, or to demonstrate the failure of a dysfunctional society whose citizens are not truly free or happy.

In seeking to understand the scale of the problems faced by human societies, and the probable risk to their continued existence, the Green Party includes an analysis both of what will happen if we don't change course and what needs to change in order to get to where we want to be. The solution must be equal to the scale of the change required. Since the scale is unprecedented, the solution must be radical.

In pronouncing our radicalism, we express our optimism in the possibility of a democratic politics worthy of the name. In spite of the current disproportional first-past-the-post electoral system, making it more difficult for Greens to get into Westminster, we enter the next general election with a real chance of electing our first Member of Parliament, Caroline Lucas. As current party leader, and since 1999 one of two serving Members of the European Parliament, Lucas has been the Greens' most recognisable public figure for well over a decade and an invaluable asset. Her media appearances are typified by keen intellect, an attention to detail, and an ability to home in on the bigger picture, if necessary by questioning the assumptions of her interviewer before putting forward the alternative Green standpoint. Lucas is passionate, resolute, and sometimes understandably impatient.

There is a tangible sense of excitement, but not complacency, in the party that we are within a whisker of gaining our first MP in Brighton Pavilion constituency. The Greens gained 22 per cent of the vote there at the 2005 general election, with candidate Keith Taylor, a Brighton councillor. A win in 2010 with Lucas will give the Party the heightened credibility it craves, with Westminster still dominating the UK political focus.

Long term

The Greens think long term, both in political outlook and electoral strategy. A win in Brighton would be important not simply for its own sake, but as a means of helping to gain additional MPs in future elections. By gaining our first MP, we would have demonstrated that we are electable at all levels of government. This would pave the way for other potential MPs and give the party as a whole a boost for the future.

Flanking Lucas on both sides are parliamentary hopefuls Adrian Ramsay in Norwich South and Darren Johnson in Lewisham Deptford. The Greens have significant councillor representation in Brighton, Norwich and Lewisham and this grassroots support has shown itself in other elections, too. The Greens have over one hundred councillors nationally, including especially good representation in Oxford, Lancaster and Kirklees, and got 1.2 million votes in the European elections in 2009.

Greens are in politics for the long haul. We have an inside joke, that if you wanted to get elected quickly you wouldn't necessarily join the Greens! However, with that commitment to radical politics comes a determination to punch above our weight when we do get elected. Since every win is hard fought, the effort of political engagement is all the greater.

When Greens get elected, people like what they see and generally come back for more. Take the 2006 local elections in London. Overnight, we went from one councillor in Lewisham to twelve across London, with representation for the first time in Camden, Islington, Hackney, Southwark and Lambeth. Moreover, the increase in elected councillors in Lewisham was nothing short of exponential, growing from one to six. In 2008, we had our first council by-election win, in the Camden ward where two Greens had been elected two years earlier, bringing our London total to thirteen.

Darren Johnson is serving his third term as a London Assembly Member and is its Chair. He was the Green's first mayoral candidate in 2000, the same year he first got elected as an AM. Johnson maintains his profile as a leading Green politician, campaigning hard for tangible green achievements within City Hall whilst holding the Mayor to account.

Johnson is also a consummate electioneer. He has been instrumental in developing party election strategy in his local borough, in the London region and nationally. When training and advising fellow activists about the importance of plugging away, and reinforcing deliveries of political literature to the electorate, he will often end his pitch with an obvious truth, accompanied by a wry smile: 'The idea is to get *more votes than the other political parties.*'

The intended irony is a reminder to activists that the *raison d'être* of a political party is to stand in order to win. But how one does justice to that win, once elected, is still up for grabs. For sure, we seek to advance our political agenda through responsible use of the office and intelligent use of the media to advertise our successes and publicise our campaigns. But the role of the Green politician is generally split between using the formal powers invested in them by office and using the political capital *informally associated* with the office to advance green politics. These aims are neither mutually exclusive nor mutually competing. To the contrary, they demonstrate what is best about green political activism, as a means of empowering ourselves and others to improve the quality of our lives.

Political capital

The idea of accumulating and spending *political capital* lies at the heart of Jenny Jones' thinking as an elected Green. Jones got elected as an Assembly Member in 2000, and has remained in office ever since. In 2004–08, during Ken Livingstone's second term as Mayor of London, Greens held the balance of power on the Assembly and made masterful use of this during the annual spending round by advancing strong green initiatives backed up with meaningful budgetary lines.

In 2003, after much debate in the London regional party, the Greens accepted an invitation from the Mayor for Jones to serve as Ken's Deputy Mayor for one year. The argument in favour hinged upon how Jones could best use the increased political resources that the office would give her. The job connoted political status in the public eye, but the aim was to deploy that capital for the advancement of green politics, not for the advancement of self. Moreover, the perception that the Greens were potentially allying themselves too closely with Ken had to be countered with the prospect that Jones would get the chance to define that relationship on her own terms. That Jones would not serve as a mouthpiece for Ken was set as a condition of acceptance.

The point about Jones's service to her party and its wider aims is worth reinforcing. Too often one gets a sense in UK politics that some, but not all, politicians are in it for personal gain or self-aggrandisement, even if they did not start out that way. The fact that Greens generally cannot take their election for granted, and might have to work harder than their political rivals in order to win, perhaps insulates them from the tendency to go into politics for selfish reasons.

However, it would be a mistake to suppose that an elected politician, including a Green, could be automatically immune to the false seductions or traps of power. To make out otherwise would be to pretend that Greens were somehow superior human beings, but that is not a credible claim. What is credible, is to promote ways of relating within a political party, and ways of forming political relationships outside of it, that have a tendency to engender and reinforce good behaviour in all. That is what I mean by value in politics.

The Green values of transparency and accountability led Jones to seek advice from her fellow members of the regional party, as one amongst equals. This kind of internal political legitimacy is becoming increasingly rare as current and past governments have often set a poor example by deciding political appointments and key diplomatic posts secretly and with the minimum of scrutiny. Who decided that Peter Mandelson deserved a job as an EU Commissioner in 2004 and why couldn't a relevant constituency have had any say in the nomination? Anyone for Baroness Ashton as the EU's High Representative? Who should decide which, if any, friends and donors deserved to be considered by the House of Lords appointments commission for a life peerage? The Greens are in favour of a fully elected second chamber, and would not preside over any snail's pace or half-baked reform.

Trust

The Green Party values the idea that decisions should be taken at the closest practical level to those affected by them. We practise this internally in order to aspire to it externally. After all, it is internally that a party has maximum control over how it organises itself and can then practise what it preaches. How can a party claim to be democratic if its leadership rules by diktat? The health of a party depends not just on both its ordinary and more prominent members having a nose for the party ethos but also in choosing to exercise that ethos, when they might have got away with doing otherwise because they were in a position to do so. With political responsibility comes accountability not just in name but *also in spirit*.

It is in the spirit of the Green Party to be *selfless* in one's politics, to put oneself to the service of others, to treat all equally. It is against that spirit, say, to take advantage of one's privileged elected position to maximise one's expenses allowances or mortgage interest claims. 2009 was a low point in UK parliamentary history, not simply in what was done by scores of MPs in order to maximise their revenue, but in what was revealed. The episode demonstrated that a political culture had been created whereby officials in the parliamentary fees office turned a blind eye to dubious expense claims made knowingly by MPs out to abuse the system. Here are some headlines concerning different MPs, from *The Daily Telegraph's* reports of the expenses scandal in May 2009: 'Blears "should be sacked for avoiding capital gains tax"' (Hazel Blears); 'The justice minister, his home and the convicted landlord' (Shahid Malik); '£50,000 to rent a cottage from his sister-in-law' (Bernard Jenkin); '£30,000 for the garden, including the ducks bill' (Sir Peter Viggers); 'The former Grenadier Guard who charged for a stainless steel dog bowl' (Mike Penning). The responsibility lies primarily with the MPs who submitted questionable claims, however imperfect the rules were or their policing.

When Hazel Blears paraded in front of the cameras with a £13,332 cheque refund for the tax office, was she motivated by genuine regret or simply ashamed that she had been found out? To make such a public display of her guilt suggests that her conscience was at best pricked only by the discovery not by the deed itself. However, in order to trust our politicians we need to know that they would act morally and honourably behind our backs, especially, not simply for fear of being found out. That requires an internal censor and a sense of self-respect.

On the eve of the 2009 European election, I was asked for an opinion on BBC News 24 on the results of a survey showing that voter trust in politicians was at an all time low, and that of all the political parties the Greens were the most trusted. Why were the Greens in such an enviable position? I answered that, for the most part, voters recognised that Greens had stuck to their principled policies on climate change long before it became popular for the other parties to start to do so. Therefore, they trusted us to say what we believed, in spite of positive or negative voter reception. This tendency to say what we believe and not to shy away from difficult truths is in short supply in political pronouncements. It is this commitment to speaking truth as we saw it, and not simply resorting to telling people what we thought they wanted to hear, that could account for our earning of trust with the electorate. Trust has to be earned over time, not just overnight.

There is a second reason why Greens might have an inbuilt advantage on the trust stakes. If I am right that we have a standing disposition to pursue long-term radical goals, with all due urgency, then those goals are underpinned by selfless values not self-serving ones. It is because we are too busy, once elected, pursuing such goals that we would not even have had time to consider self-promotion. To the contrary, attainment of our goals for the sake of humanity is our reward in itself, not the false identification of our ego with that potential success.

Calling

Contrast the Green ambition to pursue long term goals for their own sake with the apparent *ego-identification* of some mainstream politicians. Blair, under siege from reporters about the timing of his departure as PM, once evaded the question of his succession by describing the job of PM as 'not an ignoble ambition', for Gordon Brown or anyone else. This response only betrays a preoccupation with political status, not the good or harm which the occupant can use the office for.

This kind of status-anxiety is characteristic of the tradition of the aspiring politician in pursuit of their career. Wrong. For Greens, election is properly seen as a *vocation*, a calling not a career. Talk of career signals acquisition of status as a key motivation, as if your average Tory fast-tracked A-list candidate had some kind of entitlement to the position. Wrong again. Conservative and Labour party local activists are right to feel aggrieved when 'favoured' candidates get parachuted from their central offices. I cringed when someone described Greens as 'political stars of the future'. Maybe it was well intended, but such language feeds into the bogus ideology of politician as celebrity.

There is a world of difference between doing something for *its own* sake and doing something for *one's* own sake. People are quite right to feel disgust when the politicians they entrust with big decisions are apparently motivated as much or more by the ignoble ambition of minding their own comforts first, or for preying on the property market for a jackpot on the sale of their second home. There are standards in public life that need to be adhered to if we are to regain the trust in public figures that is so urgently needed. Should compliance with such standards not exactly come as second nature to a politician, then at least let it be in their better nature.

Manifesto for sustainability

Greens are naturally outward-looking, long-termist and *instinctively altruistic*. That does not mean either that we don't understand the role of selfish motivation or would seek to deprive it of all claim. But it does mean refocusing on the need to look after our planet and all the living things that depend on it, not just for our own sakes, but for the sake of other species.

A quick glance thorough the headings for the Manifesto for a Sustainable Society (or MfSS), the Green Party's most comprehensive statement of policy agenda and vision – compiled and revised by successive generations of party members, and sometimes fought over – reveals this focus on things besides ourselves. There are chapters on big political topics of the day, such as Climate Change, Economy, Education, Europe, Health, Housing, International Policy, Social Welfare and Transport, but also chapters on themes that routinely get neglected by the other parties, such as Animal Rights, Marine Industry, Natural Resources and Waste Management, Pollution and Population.

The Green's recognisable preoccupation with climate change needs dovetailing with policy on sustainable fish stocks and how to combat natural resource depletion and man-made environmental degradation. But our political vision also includes recognition of the status of non-human animals, our respect for their well-being, and the problem of unabated human population growth. What would be the environmental impact of a world population set to grow, on current trends, from 6.8 billion today to 9 billion by 2050? Would the planet be able to sustain an additional two to three billion people, many of whom might aspire to live by Western standards of consumption?

The point for now is that Greens are prepared to risk short-term unpopularity with some voters for the sake of advancing long-term goals, because we believe in the value of those goals. If the point were to get elected at all costs, Greens would not appeal to voters beyond the next electoral cycle, as they do, and Greens would not campaign for improvements in our treatment of non-human animals, as they are not eligible to vote. The point is not to get elected at all costs but to get elected *for the right reasons*.

Green radicalism is strengthened by the consistent application of human and ecological values and this allows us both to exclude less and prioritise more. Our commitment to value in politics, and optimism in the political process, asks of us that we should lead public opinion through persuasion and debate, not necessarily to be dictated by it. This returns us to the idea that voters are more inclined to trust us not simply because we sought to tell them what they *wanted* to hear, but because we sometimes told them what we thought they *needed* to hear. Politics, at its best, is also *educational*.

Public opinion

Education is a two-way street. A good political debate, for both speaker and listener, leaves us all better informed as a result. Not all public opinion is best informed just as not all public reaction is rational. Was the public grief expressed, and mobilised, in response to the death of Princess Diana rationally aware? Though I was moved to add my own flowers to the scene at Kensington Palace in 1999, I cannot discount the idea that I got caught up in a mood of generalised sentimentality.

There is a particular danger in relying on public opinion just because it might constitute a majority of opinion. That danger lies in the phenomenon of *groupthink*, the idea that people can become psychologically predisposed to believe something simply because they are around others they identify with, without proper attention to the reasons for or against that belief. Some group responses are clearly more significant than others. The laying down of flowers out of respect for the death of a public figure, whether or not one much admired either the figure or the institutions that supported and sponsored her, was probably without great political consequence. However, it could have been more consequential, in a case where group acquiescence was being sought as a means of endorsing those institutions, or of expressing allegiance to one or more sides in a dispute over the circumstances of a death.

Public or popular opinion can be a vital force in its own right, however, when it is well informed and can be mobilised for political or social or ecological good. Green campaign groups and organisations represent both a part of public opinion and an attempt to inform, extend and mobilise it. On its climate change mitigation agenda, the Green Party finds common cause with dedicated pressure groups and lobbyists in the environmental movement. Such are Friends of the Earth, Greenpeace, Climate Camp, Plane Stupid and the more amorphous Campaign against Climate Change. On its social justice and human rights agenda, the Greens find common cause with Amnesty International, Liberty, Outrage!, No2ID, Oxfam, CND, Campaign against the Arms Trade, Stop the War coalition and Unite against Fascism. On animal welfare, Greens see eye to eye with Animal Aid and the RSPCA. And on electoral reform, our ideas resonate with Make Votes Count.

These alliances, whether formal or informal, help to establish the Greens as a grassroots political organisation with a well-connected activist base. The national membership of the Green Party of England and Wales is close to 10,000 and growing, and the numbers with whom we find common cause on political campaigns is several times that again. Our agenda is influenced by these groups and our campaigns are sometimes directed through them. Many activists bring their joint membership of campaigning organisations to the attention of the party in order to identify and progress shared political aims.

In the words of the strategy section of the Philosophical Basis: 'We will even work with those who disagree with us where sufficient common ground can be found to do so. However, we do not seek power at any price, and will withdraw our support if we are asked to make irreversible or fundamental compromises.' (PB503)

It would be a mistake to suppose that for a campaigning organisation to work alongside a political party would be for them to compromise their own impartiality. Firstly, it is hard to imagine a campaign that is not political, in the broadest sense, by its seeking change through the promotion of certain values over others in the socio-political sphere. Therefore to be political is not to be automatically *party political*. Whilst it is clear that a political party may gain support by advertising its allegiance to a campaign from those who back that campaign's aims, its primary motivation for the duration of the campaign is the furtherance of those aims in a common endeavour, not the pursuit of its own vote. In so far as this common endeavour is understood and accepted, the campaign bodies need not fall foul of some tacit or explicit undertaking to remain non-party political when joining forces with a political party that shares their aims. For Greens getting elected is a means to a greater good; but where goods can be pursued independently of office, we additionally have every reason to try to do so. These means are often mutually reinforcing.

Direct action

Sometimes it may be necessary to confront an injustice by taking direct action, or civil disobedience, of a non-violent kind. The Greens endorse the intelligent use of non-violent direct action (NVDA) on a case-by-case basis, or as part of a multi-pronged political strategy, where the end justifies such means. This is a far cry from stipulating that somehow – in general – the end always justifies the means. Certainly not. It is rather to acknowledge that situations may arise in which a law helps to entrench rather than overcome a particular injustice in society, and that it can be morally justified, or even required, to break the law in order to overcome that injustice or hasten the repeal of that law. As in the Philosophical Basis: 'The Green Party does not believe there is an automatic moral obligation on all people to obey their governments[.] We believe there are occasions when individuals and groups in society may openly, and peacefully, protest at an unjust law or practice through civil disobedience.' (PB442) This is only to admit that the law as a man-made instrument is sometimes not just imperfect but badly wrong.

When, in 1955 Alabama, Rosa Parks refused to give up her seat to a white passenger, not only did she defy convention, she also inspired a boycott against a racist, oppressive rule by asserting her moral right to equal treatment. She helped give rise to the African-American civil rights movement, which eventually moved her oppressor to change for the good by granting equal access to voting and education. When an Israeli refusenik refuses to take up arms, he might rather suffer the consequences of breaking the law than see his conscience broken.

Direct action, when morally justified and intelligently applied, is a form of action that *speaks louder than words*. That is not to say that such action is always easy; on the contrary, it might require courage, resolve and the risk of unjust harm or victimisation.

Direct action can involve a person presenting themselves as a physical obstacle to the questioned authority in order to draw attention to a noble cause. In 2001, Peter Tatchell confronted Zimbabwean President Robert Mugabe in the lobby of the Hilton Hotel in Brussels, in full view of the world's media. He slipped past bodyguards in an attempt to conduct a citizen's arrest of Mugabe on charges of torture under the 1984 UN Convention Against Torture, which had been incorporated into Belgian law. However, the Belgian authorities failed to assist Tatchell in the arrest and he was badly beaten up by Mugabe's men. Still, the impact of his heroic action was to draw attention to Mugabe's human rights record.

In October 2003, Green councillor Gina Dowding was made to face a disciplinary tribunal after breaching a clause in the code of conduct under the Local Government Act 2000 regarding the disclosure of confidential information. She had decided that it was in the public interest to reveal information that she had become privy to about Lancaster City Council's decision to defer business rates payments due on British Energy's Heysham Head nuclear power station. This was an intelligent action undertaken in full knowledge of the possible repercussions, in order to expose a deal made behind closed doors that would give unfair advantage to the production of a controversial form of energy.

In November 2003, I faced a disciplinary tribunal after compromising a plan by Colin Powell, then US secretary of State for Defence, to attend an awards ceremony at my university. On the day of the proposed visit I had a letter published in the press, which advertised the contents of an internal memo indicating that staff and students were being evacuated from the library in order to adopt extensive security measures. Powell had accompanied George Bush on his controversial visit to the UK during the height of the Iraq invasion, and I had wanted to protest the suffering and death of innocents by frustrating Powell's social diary. That evening, *Channel 4 News* broke the story that Powell's visit had been cancelled for security reasons. At the subsequent tribunal, I asked, 'How for the sake of such a visit, can it be in the best interest of the university to deprive its staff and students of their educational resources for the best part of a day?' My detractors maintained that they were best qualified to judge that. But I came through; and when asked by my supporters whether I knew I would be putting my job at risk, I replied that I had no choice. (Later down the line, I got an apology from the university to say they hadn't convened the tribunal properly.)

Grassroots transition

Unthinking adoption of received opinion or submission to convention for convention's sake is a kind of groupthink that Greens like other bodies may have to confront in order to instigate radical change. The power of groupthink often lies in its ubiquity, to which anyone – including Greens – may succumb on certain days of the week. The stimulus for direct action is common to another form of grassroots mobilisation: the transition town movement. The idea is to realise a collective vision of a more sustainable society by developing local initiatives that enable people to take ever greater ownership over how they manage every aspect of their lives – from food production and purchasing patterns to energy consumption and human scale transport.

This lifestyle is hardly practised by anybody in the UK. Rather, the custom is to live in order to spend, and to outsource the production of whatever one needs or wants to specialists. No doubt, we all benefit from being able to draw upon the talents of others when everybody is better at something and none is best at everything. But the specialisation of everything has resulted in the ordinary person becoming too remote from the production of essential goods, to the extent that they would not know where to start if they were cut off from them.

The transition town movement is *counter-cultural*, as it promotes initiatives that would increase the capacity of a local community to look after its needs from within its own habitat, or in closer proximity than would otherwise be the case. By promoting local food production for example, a community can make the transition to collectively lower its carbon emissions. At the same time its inhabitants can experience the satisfaction of cooking and eating and sharing the food which they have grown for themselves through their own contact with nature, thereby increasing their well-being.

Greens are in agreement with the transition town ethos and continue to engage politically in order to improve community access to sustainable production, such as, in the case of food, the provision of allotments. The Philosophical Basis says, 'The Green Party puts changes in both values and lifestyles at the heart of the radical green agenda.' (PB001) Again, 'An ecological society will be made up of self-governing communities of a variety of sizes which will regulate their own social and economic activities.' (PB302) Transition towns engender a long-term strategy of climate change mitigation and adaptation at a local level, both by promoting carbon emission reduction and by increasing resilience to climate change impacts that would disrupt the conventional means of production or its supply chain in the not-too-distant future. Green electoral politics works hand in hand with such movements.

True politics

Let me summarise thus far. The twin aims of the Green Party are the pursuit of environmental sustainability and social justice, both through participation in the electoral process, in order to get elected to further those aims, and through grassroots campaigning with NGOs and campaign groups. The Green Party is a political party; its *raison d'être* is to stand for elections and win. But because the Green Party seeks political, social and ecological solutions fit for the scale and urgency of the challenges faced in the twenty-first century, it understands that gaining political office is not an end in itself but a vital means towards advancing its agenda. Not all politics is party politics and the Greens will work with groups which share its aims. By so doing, we reveal our commitment to, and express our optimism in, *politics worthy of the name* – both within electoral politics, despite the rules and culture we would seek to change, and by participation in social movements.

The Green Party is a *radical* party and this shows itself in the breadth of policies it would prioritise and promote, and in its manner of doing politics. We add value to politics by including consideration of non-human animals and future generations. Value enters politics also in how we stand for election, conduct ourselves when elected, and support the work of the Party. I have signalled the importance to Greens of service to society in pursuit of long-term, altruistic goals. Greens stay accountable to their members as one amongst equals, by seeking their guidance and inspiring confidence in them, to result in better-informed decisions.

We ask you to vote for us for the right reasons; not for any old reason. We seek your support for the right reasons, not at all costs. In this, we show optimism in democratic politics, treating voters as rational, intelligent adults to be persuaded one way or another.

Gandhi spoke wisely of the interdependency of means and ends: *The means is the ends in the making.* Success in our end is affected by how we choose to pursue that end. The value of our end tells us what we should be prepared to do or not do in order to achieve it – including counselling direct action. In a society free of oppression, but where lifestyle change is necessary, we try to better inform people of the facts so they can take ownership of their lives. By asking you to vote for us and our policies for the right reasons we bring you psychologically closer to helping to make the change for yourself – instead of having those policies imposed upon you without consent. We recognise the role of voter education and learn from voters ourselves.

Ken Livingstone brought in the congestion charge for London by appealing to a greater collective interest and therefore got the support of the Greens, despite some problems with the private financing of the scheme. The idea that we would all benefit from the introduction of a disincentive to drive into central London appeals to a shared idea of public good, not just individual self-interest. Reducing congestion in central London benefits passengers of both private vehicles and public transport and pedestrians and cyclists benefit from reduced traffic pollution. The initiative has helped individuals to think or behave more as citizens in a shared space and less like competitors for the finite resource of road space. Whilst you or I may feel like we are being penalised for entering a zone we could have accessed for free at the same said hour in the past, we are reconciled to everybody being required to pay the same. This, we accept, benefits everybody overall and encourages a less self-interested view of citizen interactions.

By promoting long-term, altruistic value in politics and respecting voters as thinking people, Greens engender trust in a politics worthy of the name. We are in politics for noble ends, not for ignoble personal ambition; *a calling not a career*. In the 2005 general election, I wrote, 'Greens continually challenge the lowest common denominator approach to politics by appealing to our better nature.'

Climate change

Unique selling point

People sometimes mistake us for an environmental pressure group, but we don't only care about the environment. Yet there could be worse things to be branded 'single-issue' about than the environment. It probably helps in politics, as in business, to have a unique selling point. When several political parties are competing for the attention of the voter, having a strong identity or brand can give an advantage. It matters what that brand is.

We saw why it is that Greens performed well on a poll seeking to identify which party voters trusted the most. By presenting the electorate with consistently strong policies on environmental protection and climate change over the years, and long before the other parties had started to talk about it, we may have earned a reputation for saying what we thought voters *needed* to hear, not just what we thought they *wanted* to hear. *We were believed.* The fact that the threat from climate change has become increasingly undeniable, partly through global inaction, has meant that other parties have attempted to major on this issue on a scale varying from opportunism to more or less credibility.

The suspicion of political opportunism is typified in the Conservative slogan, invented in 2006, 'Vote Blue, Go Green.' When David Cameron, in his first year as leader, spoke highly of a plan to levy new fuel taxes on flights, but his conference rejected the policy, we caught a glimpse of the underlying truth behind the rhetoric: *emptiness*. The lowest common denominator approach puts the cart before the horse, the sloganeering before the policies. Even slogans can ring true or false. Though other parties have begun to talk that talk without walking the walk, voters have drawn the implication that the Greens were right all along, and since we were campaigning on the issues long before it became popular to do so, we should be the benefactor of votes being cast for environmental reasons. The failed attempt of the Conservatives to rebrand themselves as a party for the environment has served the useful purpose of raising the political profile of the issue, probably to the advantage of the Greens. *In order to get Green, one needs to vote Green.*

Properly understood, the climate change agenda is as all-inclusive as they get. Greens have made the connection between climate change and *social justice*. Often it is those least able to afford the impact of climate change, and those least responsible for it, who are most adversely affected by it. The onset of extreme weather events, attributable to the consequences of man-made climate change, is already upon us. The World Health Organization estimates that 160,000 people already die each year through disease, drought and flooding caused by climate change. In the last decade we have witnessed, generally from the comfort of our TV screens, Hurricane Katrina in New Orleans in 1995 and, in the UK, the floods of Boscastle in 2004, Tewkesbury in 2007 and Cockermouth in 2009. Climate change mitigation needs to be at the forefront of our political agenda, an integral part of politics. Caroline Lucas has rightly criticised Cameron's attempt to don environmental clothes as a 'johnny-come-lately bolt-on environmental approach'. Meaningful action needs to happen in a substantial way, not as an optional extra.

Kyoto

Readers who follow the mainstream media will be impressed with how climate change has risen up the political agenda. This is a welcome development. But we haven't seen the concerted international legislative action that is required to begin to combat rising greenhouse gas emissions globally.

A brief overview of international climate change policy is in order, and of how it may have failed us to date. At the Rio Earth Summit in 1992, the UN inaugurated the Framework Convention on Climate Change. This established an international consensus on the need to act and put the Intergovernmental Panel on Climate Change on a secure footing as an international forum for analysis and debate of scientific findings and one of the main sources of climate change data. Climate change conferences have been held since, notably at Kyoto in 1997, where targets for emissions reductions from developed countries were set and the need for a stronger regime was flagged up. But the Kyoto protocols have been of very limited success in achieving curtailment of greenhouse gas emissions. Only a limited number of countries have participated in the framework in its most robust form, mainly from the EU, with the US absent and China (now the world's foremost emitter of CO_2) not required to do anything at all.

The emissions targets for participating countries, even on their most robust interpretation, does not include production activity, only consumption activity. This means the level of emissions reduction has been overstated. According to a calculation by Dieter Helm, after incorporating 'embedded' emissions associated with production activity of imported goods (and subtracting emissions for production of exported goods), UK emissions have increased by 19 per cent from 1990 levels (in the current accounting period, 2008–12). Kyoto would instead have us record UK emissions as showing a net decrease of 12.5 per cent, putting us ahead of its target. Nor do these targets include emissions for shipping or aviation, both of which have shown significant increases. Helm concludes that the framework has failed on both of its stated aims – committing developed countries to reducing emissions and providing a framework for going forward. Targets have been met by participating countries moving their energy-intensive production to countries like China, whose emissions have not been included at all.

Global trends in energy demand are not heading in the right direction. The International Energy Association predicts a 45 per cent increase by 2030, and even on the best scenario of rapid implementation of energy reduction initiatives, the prediction is still for a 25 per cent increase by 2030. Much of the increase in energy demand, which closely tracks carbon emissions, is predicted to come from China and India, with China currently building around two coal-fired power stations every week.

Overconsumption

At a public meeting in London, Environment Minister Ed Miliband spoke about his preparations ahead of make-or-break climate change negotiations in Copenhagen in 2009. He declared that there was no Plan B. But it was not clear he had understood the gravity of the situation faced by civilisation: the 'crapula' is already hitting the fan. He gave as an example of civic responsibility the desire of UK citizens to want to make sure that labourers producing their goods in China should be properly paid and looked after; but he ignored the fact that China was producing goods *for us for import to the UK* – therefore, we are the reason for the emissions associated with that production. There cannot be a serious attempt to combat climate change without looking to address one of its chief causes: *overconsumption*. Gandhi once said that we need to live within our means so that others may live.

The chair summarised Miliband's offerings: that he had vision; that he had political will; but did he have the toughness that would be required in the negotiations ahead? The characterisation made the audience smile, but also identified a worry with Miliband's pitch – that we could apparently carry on business-as-usual, continuing to

buy and throw away plastic and electrical goods and furniture made
in China, on demand, like there was no tomorrow. The worry that
Miliband could not walk the walk was actually revealed by his talk. His
failure to draw out the practical implications of his stated 'vision' was
not visionary nor did it demonstrate political will. I was reminded of
the lack of imagination of an 'environmental consultant' employed
by Marks & Spencer to look at the future impact of climate change
on clothing production. The representative – speaking at the launch
of a climate data resource – interpreted sustainability as the desire
to ensure that a supply of sequins for clothing imported from India
remained continuous into the future, manufactured on higher ground
if necessary.

Greens understand that changes in unsustainable consumption
are required immediately and will require leadership and vision. The
problem of climate change is made worse by an economic system
that fails to cost the impact to the environment. Patrick Geddes, a
sociologist, recognised this as long ago as 1884, when he criticised
the idea of profit as no more than 'the interest paid by nature on
the matter and energy expended upon her during the processes of
production'. He argued that economics should be redefined to take
account of the resources and energy that went into production
activities. We have long surpassed a state of nature in which we can
take as much as we want so long as we leave, in John Locke's words,
'as much and as good for all'. In 2010, scarcity not abundance is
the norm, whether we mean land, raw materials or water. Have we
learned nothing from the credit crunch? On its terms, the idea that
an economy should continue to grow year on year is ludicrous – as
if the supply of raw materials on which such growth is based were
either invariable or infinite.

The pursuit of this economic ideal for its own sake pays scant
regard to either environmental sustainability or quality of life.
Clinton's quip, 'It's the economy, stupid,' betrayed this pursuit of

a false ideal for its own sake. A UK survey showed that the more you earned, the more you couldn't afford what you thought you needed. Well, it can't be because you don't have more, since it's accepted that the more you earn the more you are able to satisfy the needs or desires you started with. The conundrum occurs because as we become richer we end up manufacturing new desires for more things, and this desire for ever greater stuff is insatiable.

Quality of life

The happiness agenda has been increasingly courted by mainstream politicians, introduced by Greens before them as the political theme 'quality of life'. The Green Party's GLA manifesto for 2004 was entitled *A Quality Life, for a Quality London.* We were ahead of the game, pursuing value-laden politics and attempting to reframe conventional political thinking.

The things that contribute to quality of life are far broader than those supposed by an economist, who treats personal well-being as the satisfaction of desire, quite irrespective of the object of that desire. Man, or woman, as *Homo economicus* is motivated by desire-satisfaction. That desire may be for a customised number plate or designer perfume. On the suitability of that thing as an object of desire, the economist will remain largely silent – by valuing each to his or her own, or to their ability to pay a price decided by the supplier and what the market will sustain. To refrain from commenting on the suitability of another's objects of desires has much to be said for it as a default assumption, but this cannot remain the final position. As a default, the idea is a libertarian one, of good heritage. John Stuart Mill, writing in *On Liberty*, understood that *the individual is generally the best judge of their interest.* Probably when individuals are left to decide they will do a better job than if somebody had decided for them.

One might suppose that the exercise of personal freedom is so commonly accepted as good, that it would take a pretty high degree of certainty about the unsuitability of somebody's desire to want to override their claim to let them decide their interest for themselves. One of the things they would lose if their freedom were restricted would be the opportunity to make their own mistakes, and to learn from them. The idea that somebody else, say the state, knew what was in your best interest smacks of paternalism, and we would want to know from what standpoint they could claim such a privileged position.

But Mill understood that situations can arise in which restrictions to personal liberty may be imposed or required under the law, and he justified this with reference to what he called the 'harm principle'. This principle allows that individuals are free to act as they please so long as they do not interfere with others to exercise their like freedoms.

For example, in the UK, the Fireworks Regulations Act 2004 prohibits the private use of fireworks between 11 p.m. and 7 a.m., except on New Year's Day, Chinese New Year, Guy Fawkes night and Diwali, when extensions are allowed. The trade off is between individuals' desires to enjoy fireworks and the wider population's desire for a decent night's sleep free from sudden or unnecessary noise, or the desire to avoid distress to animals. Identifying exceptions in the year for certain festivities allows a trade-off to be negotiated between groups with different, potentially competing interests or expectations.

We should accept that lawmakers may legitimately restrict the exercise of personal liberty, either because the individual's actions negatively impact upon another or the greater good of others; or because the individual is not acting in their own best interest, and we think intervention justified. We thereby make room for the notion of a social good which can transcend individual choice.

For Greens, quality of life assumes a difference between an

individual's assumed good when acting self-interestedly and their actual good when taken as part of the wider society or planet.

Since the more luxuries we have the more we want, shouldn't we then try to want less, over and above what we genuinely need? Greens don't pursue business-as-usual goals, where values inherent in the current economics are promoted overtly and go unchallenged by default. The status quo sees people getting increasingly miserable as they pursue materialistic goals which leave them feeling empty, whilst the society continues to exceed consumption levels that can be borne by the ecosystem or allow for future populations to be sustained.

Karl Marx once said that *the more we find value in external things the less we find value in ourselves*. He is right that accumulating stuff doesn't really make us happy, or happy in the right sort of way. Take the riots at the newly opened Ikea store in north London: people abandoned their 4x4s on the North Circular Road in order to compete for free sofas. True story. Or take the ruck outside the newly opened Primark store on Oxford Street, with people being injured. True story. These frenzies happened in the last decade and show the worst excesses of consumer culture. Retailers deliberately feed both the hype and the frenzies that follow the launch of their stores. Such scenes are hardly a sign of a society at its best. When Marx talks about the value within us, it is to such things as dignity and self-worth that he refers.

Advertising

Free sofas or cheap clothing come at a cost to the planet and the working conditions of labourers in the supply chain. Is there no governor within ourselves or in society to control our impulse to purchase more than we need? Endless adverts for sofas on television and radio assume that the only impediment to our having more is our credit rating; certainly not the long-term impact of our purchasing decisions on the Earth's finite resources and available landfill.

Green policy on advertising, in the Culture, Media and Sport section of the MfSS, contains a recognition of the negative impact aggressive commercial advertising has: 'Advertising has great impact on the world in which we live. The Green perspective is that in the context of deregulated commercial freedom and unsustainable consumption by citizens, advertising is in need of some restraint. Whilst we recognise the freedom of individuals to make informed choices for themselves, regulation is needed where the impact of consumption is to the detriment of society.' (CMS680) The point is reinforced: 'The aggregate and cumulative effect of advertising taken altogether is to increase overall demand and foster a materialist and consumption driven culture which is not sustainable. The overall volume of advertising that promotes unsustainable consumption will be controlled and gradually reduced. This control will be exercised by Ofcom.' (CMS686)

The attempt to look at some of the causes of overconsumption, in an effort to curtail it, is not a strategy you will find adopted by the other parties. But the *business-as-usual, have-your-cake-and-eat-it, laissez-faire, like-there's-no-tomorrow approach* will leave us without a habitable planet in the not-too-distant future. Greens recognise the value of exercise of free choice, but would seek to regulate the advertising that – without regard to the overall environmental impact of overconsumption – would go into conditioning, biasing or motivating those decisions. Our policy embodies a principle of harm mitigation, just like Mill. Individual businesses' advertising output doesn't operate in a vacuum, but infiltrates public or private spaces in ways that can have lasting negative social and environmental consequences. Left unchecked, current patterns of individual and social behaviour will unfairly limit the life chances of future generations and probably people around right now.

Barbara Kruger's critique of advertising in sayings such as 'I shop therefore I am' have been appropriated by the Selfridges store itself, during the sales, and taken to new levels of self-referring consumer fantasy in the process:

You want it	It's you	Buy me
You buy it	It's new	I'll change your life
You forget it	It's everything	
	It's nothing	

The context of these slogans results in their ironic teachings being turned on their head – by addressing shoppers when they are least likely to want to refrain from buying stuff, in the store itself. The shoppers are confronted by their doubts but the effect of their continued shopping is to reinforce their denial about them. Just imagine entering into a pre-emptive therapy session with your store: 'It's okay, we know how empty and conflicted you feel about hoarding all this stuff at knock-down prices, far more stuff than you need or can afford. Yes, you'll forget it! Yes, it won't change your life! Yes, it's nothing! But, don't mind me, go ahead. Shopping, not thinking defines you. Exist to shop!'

This kind of guilt-free wallowing in the having of the cake and eating it might be clever and existentially comforting, but it does not help to steer us away from highly consumptive patterns of behaviour which are contributing to the destruction of the planet. Not funny, is it?

New Deal

It isn't funny also that instead of using a credit-fuelled deep recession as a warning about the bankruptcy of the economic model, and opportunity for systemic reform, this government would instead pursue short-term initiatives in an effort to make short-term economic gains. The government's car scrappage scheme is an example of this short-termist ideological thinking. Instead of seeking to retrain and redeploy car workers in sustainable green industries – workers who would otherwise face involuntary redundancy – this government would rather subsidise an unsustainable industry, based on the false ideology of continuous growth. Car owners are encouraged to trade in their old cars for new at a discount to both retailer and consumer. During its period of operation, one-fifth of all new cars were bought under the scheme. Unfortunately, such programmes not only serve to prop up a failing sector of the economy, but represent a double blow to the environment.

It is probable that for the majority of vehicles traded in under the scheme the environmental impact would have been less if the new car had not been built and the older car had been maintained; even after taking fuel economy into account. Retrofitting old cars with better fuel technology is also an option. Instead, this government has sought to incentivise our purchasing decisions to encourage greater consumption and waste.

Greens recognise the value of meaningful work, both to the worker and the wider society, and would adopt a 'Green New Deal' – a radical programme of action put forward by a working group of environmentalists, energy experts and financial reformers in 2008, and inspired by Roosevelt's New Deal of the 1930s – by investing in a new low carbon economy. The measures would involve: the reform of international finance; an end to subsidies for coal and nuclear power; and the roll out of a large-scale programme of public and private investment in renewable energy and energy efficiency. The latter would see the creation of hundreds of thousands of new green jobs.

The Green New Deal group correctly characterised the global economy at this time as in the throes of a 'triple crunch', resulting from the combined impact of a credit-fuelled financial crisis, accelerating climate change and increased energy insecurity, a context with no real precedent. In an attempt to galvanise politicians into action, the group, which included the Greens' Caroline Lucas, drew a parallel with the unprecedented nature of President Roosevelt's '100 days of lawmaking' as a response to the Great Depression.

Indeed, we have witnessed how financial institutions and banks such as Enron, Lehman Brothers, Icesave and Northern Rock collapsed, leaving investors, and especially depositors facing huge financial losses, with only very limited access to information about the true scale of the financial risks their banks were taking with their money. We have learned how dubious financial practice, or malpractice, resulted in lending banks buying and selling financial products that had traditionally been the preserve of investment banks – even assuming they were legitimate for any bank to do.

The so-called 'sub-prime' mortgage market originated in the US and enabled first-time house buyers to own their own home with minimal quality assurance procedures (like self-certification), and allowed a widening gulf to be created between the deposit and the ability of the buyer to make good on the purchase through future earnings. Some sub-prime financial products (now notorious) consisted of little more than pieces of paper containing mathematical formulae that would have been indecipherable to layperson and financial adviser alike. It is no wonder that when the penny dropped – or when a critical mass of individuals sought to make good on their investment in surreal sub-prime products – that a collapse in the system ensued; finding its way back to the private depositor, whose monies had been raided by the bank in order to engage in financial speculation, against traditional savings bank ethos.

Green economics would seek to re-establish the linkage between the value of a currency and what real value was used to back that currency up. The value of a sub-prime mortgage product is both too abstract and too unrelated to the actual value said to accrue over time when cashing in on the product. Suppose that it costs x amount to build a house in a particular location with particular materials and labour. One scenario is that the price of the house will rise year on year due to increased scarcity of materials and land in relation to a rising population, or even due to desirability of location in relation to local amenities and beauty spots. However, it seems that the rises in house prices well beyond inflation seen in the UK in recent decades were premised on an exaggerated valuation, disproportionate to the true rise in the asset's value. When so much of the credit-fuelled UK economy – including Treasury and Bank of England regulatory decisions – is historically based on a projected rise in house prices that bears little resemblance to true value, it should come as no surprise when the whole fiscal edifice comes tumbling down before our eyes.

The economics section of the MfSS contains a statement about the impact of bad financial practice and the need to overcome this through reform: 'Greed-driven lending and financial engineering lead to the accumulation of debts, derivatives and other securities based on debt, and so to financial crises.' (EC662) In particular, Greens would avoid: excessive economic dependence on private debt; the reliance of banks on interbank lending rather than customer deposits; excessive lending on mortgages; complex or opaque financial instruments; and lax or inadequate official regulation. Instead, a Green government would establish a network of local Community Banks – democratically accountable non-profit-making trusts – in order to support the growth of local and regional economies and increase democratisation of the banking system. Such banks, with the support of the local community, would be entitled to create their own local currencies, to operate alongside the national one.

The solution does, in part, lie in the economy; but in its root and branch reform, not with tinkering around the edges. Therein lies *the economy, stupid, not the stupid economy*. The Green New Deal proposal seeks to address the twin emergencies of climate change acceleration and depleted fossil fuel supplies within the framework of a re-regulated financial order.

Emergency

It is difficult to overstate the potential impact of climate change in the future, if left unmitigated. In its 2001 assessment report, the IPCC predicted that under a business-as-usual scenario global mean temperature will rise between 1.4°C and 5.8°C by the end of this century. Subsequent research by the Hadley Research Centre, based at the UK Meteorological Office, estimated a rise of up to 8°C over the same period, again on present trends. On either scenario, the resulting rise in sea levels would devastate Bangladesh and put low-lying cities like Shanghai, New York, Mumbai and London at risk, leaving behind up to 200 million environmental refugees by 2050.

The true risks are greater again than those forecast by many climate models, once positive feedback mechanisms are taken into account. Such mechanisms are generally not sufficiently well described to be included in the models, but have been held responsible by different groups of scientists for abrupt changes in climate in the past. For example, the UK, relative to our latitude, benefits from the warming effect of the Gulf Stream, which acts like an ocean temperature conveyor belt on our shores: the disruption or diversion of the stream by freshwater melting off the Greenland ice sheet could plunge us into sudden and lasting sub-Arctic temperatures all year round. Other possible scenarios include the temperature-induced rapid collapse of the Amazon rainforest and an exaggerated rise in temperature due to the release of methane gas, a more potent greenhouse gas than CO_2, from both continental shelves under the ocean and melting Siberian permafrost.

The Arctic polar ice is also melting at an alarming rate. At a given time of year, it is now half the size it was in the 1960s and 1970s. James Balog, a nature photographer of some thirty years, has produced a twenty-minute presentation recording the extent of glacier retreat, captured through time-lapse photography as part of the Extreme Ice Survey. He helps us to grasp the sheer magnitude of the ice losses involved by superimposing iconic images of Capitol Hills or double-decker buses on to photographs of receding ice sheets. The iconic images are instantly recognisable singly and in close up but once superimposed on to the face of the retreating glacier, after getting lined up end to end and stacked on top of one another, they end up both multiplied and miniaturised. The fictional image of thousands of buildings being lost to the ocean is almost as spectacular as the sight of the glacier retreat itself, and we are left under no illusion of the scale of the problem in real-time and the need to address it urgently.

This attempt by Balog to get us to internalise the environmental facts of our situation by intelligent use of imagery is also deployed in the films *An Inconvenient Truth* (with Al Gore) and *The Age of Stupid* (by Franny Armstrong). Gore ends his series of Powerpoint presentations with a scene of a river bank and stream, offered up to the viewer as an aspect of natural habitat at great risk of ruin. We don't want to lose this, do we? So we are supposed to think, and feel. Therefore, individual action must follow. Unfortunately, little short of global stasis has followed.

Age of Stupid

Armstrong's film is more telling as a piece of movie-making, making deeper interconnections between economic injustice and climate injustice; but that's hardly sufficient in itself to bridge the gulf between recognition and collective action. The film is alarming, and rightly so – but not alarmist. That's the difference between telling it as it is, which it does, and overstating the case with intent to shock. How could it have been responsible for the film to have deliberately understated the case for fear of making people afraid otherwise? That isn't to say that the future scenario depicted isn't shocking – but then so is the current world on which it is based; if we choose not to look away.

The Age of Stupid goes beyond *An Inconvenient Truth* in simply communicating facts well. Armstrong tries to get us to internalise those facts in a way that weighs on our conscience – by appealing not just to our reason but to our imagination. When we hear the stories of our contemporaries – through the fictional device of a future archivist – perhaps we can better see where we are headed on the business-as-usual scenario. Perhaps we can be made to look back on ourselves, as we are living now, through the lens of Pete Postlewaithe's archivist?

Our contemporaries depicted in the film are well chosen. Jay is an entrepreneur and fancies himself as a philanthropist, starting up a low-cost airline in India for the good (so he thinks) of his fellow people. By moving day workers off publicly run trains on to privately run planes, Jay will be contributing to a net increase in greenhouse gas emissions. The negative impact of his enterprise on the environment, in his lifetime, relative to the good he thinks he is doing (also in his lifetime) seems to him militated against, if it isn't lost on him. We witness the distress of a wind turbine architect – who would have his family sacrifice their holiday abroad to limit their carbon emissions – lose his planning application to a well-organised group of local objectors. We hear one of the objectors acknowledge the threat from climate change whilst, in the same breath, revelling in her victory over the architect.

These stories are meant to teach us that we cannot both have our cake and eat it. At least, not those particular slices. If workers and entrepreneurs alike realise that faster transport is not necessarily better, when the environment is factored in, or local residents realise that autonomy of energy supply is in their greater interest, then we will have moved towards more sustainable slices of cake.

I participated in a panel discussion of the film, in which members of the audience expressed mixed reactions. None was left indifferent, but the mixture of responses probably reflected the different times at which people were coming to the issue, either for the first time or after more or less sustained and prior engagement with the issue. One filmgoer was vocal in his frustration (even anger) that our politicians, as he put it, were not doing more to combat the problem that he had just been introduced to and had found so compelling. Others were somewhat less shocked by the film, either because they had already explored and been impressed by the climate science behind the film or had drawn similar conclusions already about the twin needs for concerted international action and for individuals in the developed West to voluntarily cut back on overconsumption and carbon emissions. On average, it is true, there are huge international variations on how much CO_2 each person emits. In 2000, the US averaged 20 tonnes of CO_2 emissions per person, the UK 9, China 2.5 and Africa 1 tonne. Out of the 5 tonnes emitted by the average global citizen, 4 resulted from fossil fuel consumption.

Others again showed all the signs of feeling dispirited or demotivated. Unfortunately, this is not an uncommon response in wider society and many Green candidates have faced potential voters who have complained either about the sheer magnitude of the collective task before us, as global citizens; the futility of their individual actions against the backdrop of widespread environmentally unconscientious behaviour; or the difficulty of telling, in some objective sense, whether so much damage has already been done that the situation can no longer be recovered from. Whilst these are big thoughts for anybody to be having, about the continued existence or otherwise of the human race and other planetary species – that cannot be wholly resolved in a book purporting to tell people why they should vote Green – let me nonetheless attempt to sketch out a partial answer to these grave worries.

Self-interest and altruism

Part of the answer lies in a better understanding of how people, as a collective, can be led to better act in their genuine self-interest. Here are three ways.

Firstly, a person can do things which they can come to regret as against their better interest or even against their interest at the time at which they do it. A standard example is the smoker who wishes to give up and is therefore conflicted about smoking, but still craves the tobacco, whether or not they get pleasure from it any longer. Smokers can give up, either through willpower, through medical assistance, or through group solidarity with others. When they do succeed it will likely be through replacement of one pattern of behaviour with another, which they overall accept and prefer as in their better interest; with the likelihood that as the new habit forms, it will become easier for them to resist the craving, until the craving becomes only a mild temptation or distraction. This is not to deny that many people choose to smoke and neither feel conflicted about it nor wish to give up nor should wish to give up. We should not be prepared to say that, all things considered, each and every person should give up smoking. We are all individuals with our own needs and purposes, and it would be foolish to suppose that such a claim, whilst true for the most part, could not be without plenty of exceptions. In the movie *Pitch Black*, Lewis Fitzgerald's character, Paris, stranded on a hostile moon, reaches for his cigar and quips, 'It's amazing how one can do without the necessities in life, so long as one has life's little luxuries.' We may all wish to have our treats. We eat in order to live, not live in order to eat. But always?

For the purposes of social policy, however, we recognise that the cost to the National Health Service of treating smoking-related diseases is so great that it has a disproportionate impact on funding for other front-line medical emergencies and ways should be found to inform and advise the general population about the risks to health through habitual smoking. Measures could extend to a ban on the promotion of tobacco products through advertising or sponsorship, but not to their actual sale. When the Labour government instigated a smoking ban in pubs and clubs, this predictably caused consternation amongst some; but many smokers accept or even applaud the idea that they should not be entitled to degrade the air of those around them or to raise others' health risks through involuntary passive smoking.

The second way in which a person can be led to better act in their self-interest is to recognise that often, by cooperating with others, the good to each overall will be greater than it would have been otherwise. Economists and moral philosophers have long understood the limitations of purely 'self-interested' rationality in directing an individual to the best outcome. The prisoners' dilemma is a story that helps us to understand our rational limitations.

Suppose two inmates are guilty as charged, but from the confines of their separate prison cells are asked to confess. Each knows that they can optimise their chances of release by having the other charged alone. But if each seeks to implicate their accomplice, they will both end up with the maximum sentences. By pursuing their self-interest autonomously, without regard to the other, they will both end up worse off. Therefore, they need to accept that the best they can do in that situation is to remain silent both about their own involvement and the other's. Then they will each get a much smaller sentence. But this outcome can generally only be obtained if they decide to cooperate; or in absence of the ability to confer, elect to trust one another not to shop the other.

The idea of cooperation means the resident who would abstain from recycling for fear that nobody else on his street would pull their weight, can be made to participate, knowing that if everybody sacrificed a little time and energy then the lot of everybody is improved. In the long term, the alternative course of inaction by all means everybody would suffer worse consequences.

The third way in which a person can be led to better act in their self-interest is through the idea of a collective goal or social good. This is a potentially more transformative idea, which resonates both with the assumption that the Green Party pursues value in politics and with the claim that people can be *altruistically* motivated. Voters who dismiss the suggestion that people can act out of a desire to help others are sometimes led astray by the seductive idea that individuals act, and only ever act, out of self-interested motivation.

I take the idea that human beings are intrinsically selfish to be false. But we should try to understand why, in order to remotivate some of the filmgoers and voters left overwhelmed by the climate change challenge.

Abraham Lincoln was himself seduced by the idea that all human beings are motivated purely by self-interest, or prompted by selfishness when doing good. He once debated the proposition with a friend on a coach journey. As they crossed a bridge, Lincoln asked the driver to stop so he could rescue some piglets from the river below. The sow was also in distress, before he returned her offspring to the safety of the bank. When later challenged by his companion on the demonstrable selflessness of his behaviour, Lincoln replied, 'Why, bless your soul, that was the very essence of selfishness. I should have had no peace of mind all day had I gone on and left that suffering old sow worrying over those pigs. I did it to get peace of mind, don't you see?'

Lincoln was wrong about the motive for his action. He had confused the desire to do good for its own sake with the fact that the desire was had by him. The fact that all desires are had by somebody does not mean that some desires can't be better than others by having as their objects something or somebody other than oneself. A desire to help oneself is different from a desire to help another, even if one were to derive pleasure or satisfaction from acting on the desire to help another, and did in fact succeed in that. The success would lie in the assistance received, not the feelings associated with the desire, which are secondary. Moreover, the fact that we may derive satisfaction from helping others cannot only help to reinforce our motivation for doing good but can lead us to do more good than we would have done otherwise. Rather than the psychological component of the action undermining the good, it can serve to complement it.

We now answer the sceptic about our human ability to overcome the climate change challenge in one of three ways: (a) that it is in their individual self-interest; (b) it is in their individual self-interest to cooperate; and (c) that it is in their interest to pursue the good of others besides themselves, whether they directly or indirectly benefit.

Global warming deniers

This kind of scepticism about human motivation, thus characterised, is far removed from the kind of unscientific scepticism that gets over-represented in the news media as a live question – that man-made climate change is somehow a false hypothesis. I intend to spend next to no time dismissing the bad reasoning which gives rise to wholesale scepticism about climate science. A sceptical disposition has a vital role to play in good scientific enquiry, but not when it becomes intransigent, which is then a form of denial. Deniers are guilty of hiding their heads in the sand, whilst both the scientific evidence, and the scientific and popular consensus associated with it, grows and becomes insurmountable. The idea that climate change is happening, yet human beings have not been responsible for the rapid and accelerating trends in carbon and temperature (which correlate with the industrial and post-industrial revolution) is hardly less incredible than the idea that climate change is not happening at all. Neither is a credible claim, and each is answerable to the probability of the contrary hypothesis, that human beings have had, and are continuing to have, a highly negative impact on the biosphere; which, if left unchecked, will lead to our extinction.

Sceptical doubt about our ability to overcome the real challenge of climate change is a far more credible concern, which raises questions about the exercise of altruistic human motivation. I have argued that other-regarding motivation and action is both possible and, for Greens, an essential component of a value-laden political process worthy of the name.

Contraction and convergence

At an event in 2005 in City Hall, Ken Livingstone was asked about our chances of combating climate change. He answered, perfunctorily, that it was already too late. He went on to offer us some positive ideas and I would suggest that, far from resigning himself to a fatalistic consequence, Ken had demonstrated a commitment to political value that signalled hope in triumph over adversity, instead of despair.

I can't answer for Ken whether he literally thought it was too late, but I do think this is a question the reader may wish to dwell on. It's not a question, I would suggest, that we find it easy to get our heads round. Bertrand Russell, when discussing the madness of using nuclear weapons, wryly observed, 'There is nothing worse than universal death.' Yet still the US, UK, France, Russia, China, Israel, India, Pakistan and North Korea have amassed enough weapons to wreak mass destruction upon the human population not once but many times over. It seems there *is* something worse than universal death, and that would be to destroy the integrity of the planetary ecosystem and all the plant and animal life which it sustains. Runaway climate change could have just this kind of catastrophic effect. If civilisation has shown itself so inadequate at ridding itself of such destructive weapons, with what confidence can we expect to rid ourselves of the threat from man-made climate change?

So-called 'mutually assured destruction' (MAD) has been used as an attempt to justify a state of affairs that had already been reached: the status quo of non-disarmament is apparently logical *because* no state would want to enter into a nuclear exchange which neither side could win. But that's hardly rational, since it ignores the preferable alternative of having no such weapons in the first place, a standpoint from which the risk of wars that nobody allegedly wanted could be returned to close to zero. The analogy with climate change seems to be that if no state wanted to pursue a unilateral policy of radical emissions abatement because this was not being pursued multilaterally, then mutual destruction would be assured. However, the disanalogy is that such mutual destruction is no longer hypothetical, but actual. Unfortunately, war is already being waged on the biosphere, so inaction leaves us perfectly vulnerable to the cumulative impact of our emissions.

The Green Party advocates 'contraction and convergence' as the international framework for getting to the required destination in response to climate change. That would allow for a smooth and equitable transition to a safe level of global CO_2 emissions resulting from human activity. In the Climate Change section of the MfSS, these terms are spelled out: 'Contraction means adopting a scientifically determined safe target concentration level and setting global annual emissions levels which should take the atmosphere to that target [. . .] Convergence means taking the world in an achievable way, both technically and politically, from the present situation to a common level of per-capita emissions in a target year.' (C222–3)

Within this scheme, Greens would seek to implement tradable carbon quotas nationally. The government would allocate everybody a monthly carbon allowance free of charge and some trading of carbon would be allowed if some sought to use others' remainders, subject to availability. The total amount would be capped and reduced annually – as per the principles of contraction and convergence – to help us reach a 90 per cent reduction from 1990 levels by 2030. The Green Party reduction is more ambitious, in both total reduction and time-scale, than the government's target of 60 per cent by 2050. The Greens require a 10 per cent reduction per year instead of 2 per cent. We would pursue this immediately, seek to discourage countries from trailing or abstaining and lead by example. Anything less would simply assure our mutual destruction.

Demotivation

We still need to finally answer the demotivated filmgoers and voters. I fear even Greens risk underestimating the psychological component of the challenge. I already described our approach to the political process as inherently optimistic. Some may wish to accuse us of naivety. But the reason for our optimism is not wishful thinking but objectivity about the scale of the challenge and the *inestimable loss* that would be brought about through inaction. It's possible to be objective not just about facts, but about values, too. Greens' optimism results from a sense that human beings and the biosphere are of inestimable value and that since we have shown ourselves to be capable of making progress, as a civilised society, in abolishing slavery or giving women the vote, for example, then further transformation is not just possible but necessary. We're not subjectivists about the value of human beings and other things. That is to say, we don't think it's up to you, or up to me, what value the continued existence of the human race and planetary species has, or that we could both be right about such value even if we contradicted one another. Such value is to be found out there in the world, for us to discover. For sure, we say it has positive value, both from the standpoint of Greens and as human beings.

I argued that Greens could jolt some people out of their doubt that human beings would be able to meet the climate change challenge by pointing to a transformed idea of the other-regarding values; one that can motivate. Yet there are further reasons why people may remain recalcitrant to this appeal, either because they are subjectivists about value or because they are in some sense predominately self-seeking. It should be possible to educate those who start out as subjectivists about value that the world they inhabit is really with value, one way or another, quite independently of their own reckoning of the matter. Therefore, the fact that two people might violently disagree about the permissibility of slavery does not mean that one of them is not mistaken. When Gandhi quipped, 'What do I think about Western civilisation? I think it would be a good idea,' he didn't assume progress to be impossible.

The predominately self-seeking mindset is unfortunately prevalent in society and this is where Greens may underestimate the scale of the challenge. Self-seeking tends to culminate in the pursuit of short-term pleasure, simple pleasures or avoidance of pain at all costs. We all know what it means to pursue such pleasure, but it is clear that the ills of overconsumption cannot be abated without learning to moderate our pleasures. A mobile phone ad says 'impatience is a virtue' in order to feed the consumer fantasy that you can have your cake and eat it like there's no tomorrow; to get people to feel that what they already have is obsolete so that they will want to try new things. Why make do with DVDs when you can have Blu-Ray? This government has also pursued a media policy which extols the value of inbuilt redundancy. Under such policy, we would be destined to have our TV sets rendered obsolete overnight because we'd need new digital televisions to view the digital broadcasts. In a telling admission, UK market researcher Verdict said, 'The electricals market is highly cynical and relies on exciting new products capturing the consumer imagination to drive growth.'

Self-pity

The self-seeking mindset comes into its own in the unconscious. When George and Laura Bush implored the citizens of the United States not to let their children watch the US bombings of Iraq in 2003, for fear of upsetting them, did this not put the displeasure of watching news footage ahead of the displeasure, or downright death, meted upon innocent Iraqis by the head of state? Unfortunately, some of those demotivated by the climate change challenge also seem to want to put the unpleasantness of the fate ahead of taking responsibility for it. Greens are also inclined to want to divert attention away from the unpleasantness of the fate, not because they don't wish us to take collective responsibility for it, but because they fear the demotivatory response. That's a reasonable fear, because the response is a real psychological one, that only adds to the challenge.

In so far as there is a mean to be struck in communicating the climate change challenge, I would counsel different strokes for different folks. When meeting with schoolchildren doing a project on the threat from climate change, at the bank of the Thames Barrier, I could point to the river without seeking to patronise them by supposing that they shouldn't want to be alerted to the threat from flooding. For practical tips in the home, I said, one could boil only as much water as one needed for a tea, switch appliances off properly, and lodge a water buoy in the flush cistern, to name a few. One wouldn't want to do nothing for fear of not being able to do everything.

Yes, standing for election as a Green, there can be a tendency to want to focus on positive ways forward and to underestimate the threat of failure. But the threat of failure, for some, is probably a great, if sometimes unconscious motivator. When Pete Postlewaithe asked, at the end of *The Age of Stupid*, whether we didn't in some sense think we weren't worth saving, he invited us to reflect on the resolve we would need to overcome the threat. This is *soul-searching*. When confronted by voters who find the threat from the challenge too grim to want to face up to, let's use the *Age of Stupid* worker in sub-Saharan Africa as our inspiration. She was barely making enough money to be able to save for a university education, but that was her goal. It's not amazing how one can do without the little luxuries in life, when one is too busy trying to safeguard the necessities.

The Western, post-Freudian psychological reaction that would put dread or self-pity about the climate change fate ahead of the person's responsibility for that threat should be neutralised head on. We start by recognising it for what it is. To really care about the world we leave behind, would be to focus less on our current motivations and more on where we need to get to; and let the motivation find itself. Soul-searching complete, we need to be outward directed, not narcissistic.

Reawakening

Let us begin to draw this chapter on climate change to a close by reviewing what we learned and looking again at the idea of ecological value. We said that voters recognised the Greens as the strongest party for action on the environment, but this was part of a holistic agenda which took in social justice as a core aim. We looked at the international framework for dealing with climate change legislation, and its gross limitations. We saw how overconsumption both contributed to environmental degradation and ended up leaving consumers far less happy than they would have imagined. We saw how quality of life goals were unashamedly twisted by aggressive advertising. Greens would redress that imbalance through a massive programme of investment in renewable energy and energy efficiency, with the twin goal of retraining workers in sustainable industries.

We looked at how film and documentary makers had sought to raise awareness of the climate change emergency and how a variety of more or less rational responses could be had. In particular, we addressed doubts about our ability to overcome the climate change challenge, saying that human beings could be motivated through cooperation and altruism in the service of non-selfish goals. Greens advocated contraction and convergence as the international framework for advancing global mitigation and the need for the UK to adopt stronger targets than pronounced by this government, as backed up by the science. We discussed how the Greens' inherent optimism in the political process must not deter us from facing up to the hidden challenge of a Western personality which often puts avoidance of uncomfortable feelings ahead of resolution of difficult truths.

Unfortunately, avoidance of uncomfortable feelings or fear itself can sometimes result in irrational responses. At the height of the New Orleans emergency following Hurricane Katrina in 2005, instead of state and citizen pulling together, suspicion was the order of the day. Basic necessities like food and shelter were in short supply and evacuation was required, but police and troops sought to find suspected looters instead. In the words of Louisiana Governor Kathleen Blanco, 'Three hundred of the Arkansas National Guard have landed in the city of New Orleans. These troops are fresh back from Iraq, well trained, experienced, battle tested and under my orders to restore order in the streets. They have M-16s and they are locked and loaded. These troops know how to shoot and kill and they are more than willing to do so if necessary and I expect they will.' (ABC News)

Only in a more advanced state of civility can we overcome

the illegitimacy of the fear response. Later on, we will outline the Green position on use of lethal force by police or army. For now, let's recognise that our collective ability to come together in times of emergency resulting from climate change-related events is wanting. Some might suppose that things will get worse before they get better. The thought is that emergencies of sufficient magnitude or frequency will eventually jolt people into meaningful action on climate change mitigation. But who's to say that things won't simply get worse before they became intolerable? Without political leadership and reform of unsustainable ways of living, in our lifetimes, the outlook is not promising. Green politics is part of this solution and the idea of ecological value may help to overcome our anthropocentric ways of thinking along the way.

Bill Devall and George Sessions, authors of *Deep Ecology*, propose two such ecological principles: 'Self-realisation: persons will grow and mature through a new and deeper understanding of their place in the natural world; and biocentric equality: a denial of the privileged status of human life.' They believe that living by the second principle leads to greater preservation and restoration of the natural world. It isn't necessary for ecologists or Green politicians to hold to such principles, but it's clear that belief in them could help to inform a Green political outlook and lead others to reflect upon or engage in environmental initiatives when they otherwise might not.

Environmental belief

In 2009, in a landmark decision, Tim Nicholson, an employee of property firm Grainger, won a court ruling entitling him to have his belief in the importance of acting on climate change classified as a philosophical belief for the purpose of anti-discrimination protection under the 2003 Religion and Belief Regulation. The case came about because Nicholson had been dismissed by his employer after protesting about being ordered by his boss to make a special flight (which he took) from London to Ireland in order to personally deliver a Blackberry device that had been left behind in the office by his boss. Mr Justice Michael Burton ruled that, 'A belief in man-made climate change, and the resulting moral imperatives, is capable if genuinely held, of being a philosophical belief for the purpose of the 2003 Religion and Belief Regulations.'

This is not to say that such belief is tantamount to religion. The reason why environmental belief was included as a set of possible beliefs to which such protections could be afforded is because, like religious *or* philosophical beliefs, they may satisfy the requisite criteria for belief worthy of the name. Justice Burton outlined five such criteria: that the belief must be genuinely held; as belief not opinion; regarding a substantial aspect of human life; serious, cogent and important; and worthy of respect in a democratic society and compatible with others' fundamental rights. One should not confuse the idea that environmentally held beliefs and religious beliefs may hold this much in common with the idea that such beliefs share a common evidential base or none.

For sure, many, if not most environmentalists will base their beliefs, in part, on scientific and empirically observable data about climate change and the need to tackle it. They may even discount religious belief as highly dogmatic and evidentially unproven or unprovable. Therefore, it is ironic for them to enjoy legal protection for their beliefs on grounds that they shared other features in common with religious beliefs, whilst they differed in one of the most important sources for their beliefs, their evidential bases or none.

Environmentalists should be prepared to counsel that their beliefs were grounded in deeply held beliefs, worthy of the philosophical claim. As ably articulated by Nicholson in response to the ruling: 'It is the moral and ethical values that I hold that have motivated me to action on climate change and these moral and ethical values are similar to those promoted by the world's major religions [but] based on scientific evidence, not faith or spirituality.' Counsel for the employee, Dinah Rose QC also summed up the ruling beautifully: 'The philosophical belief in this case is that mankind is headed towards catastrophic climate change and that, as a result, we are under a duty to do all that we can to live our lives so as to mitigate or avoid that catastrophe for future generations. It addresses the question, what are the duties that we owe to the environment and why?'

Observance of a duty could mean that requesting a man to make a special trip, at some cost to the planet, to correct for the oversight of his employer should be refused. Once Nicholson's boss had forgotten his device, through no fault of anybody but himself, then it would offend against environmental duty to expect somebody to rescue the situation by hand-delivering it to him. That the employee also took exception to the request, and saw that it contravened the company's own environmental policies, only *aggravated* the offence.

Environmentalists have every reason to celebrate this ruling – and little to fear from it other than misinterpretation – since it recognised environmental belief as worthy of serious, credible and cogent assent; which indeed it is. It might be improper to class environmental belief as the 'new religion', but it certainly can show itself to be sufficiently weighty to merit prioritisation, and indeed protection, ahead of competing values and claims for action that would otherwise frustrate those environmental ends. This ruling should help others to see that. We do face an unprecedented challenge, for the first time in human civilisation. New values may need to be promoted and enforced, or rather values as old as creation itself may need to be rediscovered.

Transformative experience
The first astronauts were prevented from speaking about their

transformations by their space agencies, so published their thoughts independently. Aleksandr Aleksandrov, of the former USSR, wrote, 'We are all children of the Earth. It does not matter what country you look at. We are all Earth's children, and we should treat her as Mother.' Edgar Mitchell, of the US, wrote, 'On the return trip home, gazing through 240,000 miles of space towards the stars and the planet from which I had come I suddenly experienced the universe as intelligent, loving and harmonious.'

Aleksandrov's sentiment mirrors the idea of scientist James Lovelock of the Earth as a single, holistic system – Gaia or Mother Earth – which is self-regulating, and in which we human beings are just part of a wider whole, as if implicated in a wider nervous system. By working against nature, rather than in harmony with it, we represent dysfunction and disturbance away from the whole. By *reframing* our conception of ourselves, we can aim to restore balance to the system, working in concert with nature not against it. These are ecocentric rather than anthropocentric ideas. Mitchell's transformative experience is also premised on a sense of the wider whole, this time visually impressed upon him by the self-identity of planet Earth in relation to the rest of the universe.

Imagine. No, really imagine, being cast into deep, predominately empty space; then being brought back from the emptiness to the magnificence of planet Earth in all its variety and complexity, all its precious, barely intelligible, processes of life and regeneration. Does not this reality command the deepest awe and respect for our planet? Life is rich.

Suppose we co-exist with the planet, as a speck in the vast emptiness of space; does this not make us feel both small but mightily privileged? How does the 'I Shop therefore I am' sign look to Mitchell gazing through 240,000 miles of space back at Earth? Answer: human beings shoplifting the planet.

When Postlewaithe the archivist presses the button to start the transmission of untold stories into deep space, are we not saddened by the thought that we have lost the plot, that our best hope is for another life form to discover our fate – not to save us, but for them to laugh, cry or pity us?

What futile hope is this in relation to the chance we still have as living, vital beings – cognisant of our man-made destructive ways and in command of our own destinies – to save ourselves and our family of planetary species?

Greens are passionately committed to the future sustainability of the Earth, but we need everybody to be signed up to this; for us to have a fighting chance of survival.

This is a calling, not a career.

A just society

Greens believe in equality: we act to promote it; we fight to combat inequality. As politicians and activists, we legislate, lobby and campaign to ensure that people are not discriminated against on the basis of gender, ethnicity, sexuality, disability, age, or religious belief (or none). We advance policies which promote, maintain and protect fundamental freedoms and rights.

One size does not fit all: sometimes one has to weigh up competing claims for finite resources and adjudicate between them. In a just and equitable society the basic needs of food, housing and health must be provided for all. This is non-negotiable. Basic needs are what each and every one of us must have in order to sustain a minimally decent existence. The Green Party's Philosophical Basis expresses this as, 'Every person, in this and future generations, should be entitled to basic material security as of right.' (PB001)

Beyond this, we believe in a right to a decent education and the guarantee that people are treated fairly by legal and state institutions. Our institutions must be run along democratic principles that promote equality of opportunity, fair access to resources, and dignified outcomes. Institutions which propagate false hierarchy and damage or subvert those ends will be abolished or reformed.

Through progressive policies Greens seek to promote quality of life beyond narrow economic indicators. The core principles say, 'The success of a society [. . .] should take account of factors affecting the quality of life for all people: personal freedom, social equity, health, happiness and human fulfilment.'

We recognise our increased responsibility to those beyond our shores, because of the negative impact of a dysfunctional economic system on people producing for us abroad, and because we have an obligation to house and look after those fleeing persecution in war-torn situations. We work to promote just international institutions and instruments that will assist countries to maintain good relations and we will pursue violators of human rights in the international courts.

Basic income

Greens believe that the most vulnerable in society should be assisted by all. To do less would be unjust: it is our *duty* to help those in need. A Green government would instigate reform of the welfare state in order to improve the lot of everybody, taking personal and social well-being as the goal.

We are *welfare socialists*: we believe in the role of the welfare state and the need for a guaranteed welfare for each and every citizen or dependant. This is achieved, in part, by allocation and collection of taxes, followed by the just distribution or redistribution of revenue to people and service providers.

Greens are also *eco-socialists*: we are committed to evaluating the cost of things to the earth, as we seek to recalibrate our goals with respect to overall habitability and quality of life. But Green politics is not primarily about identifying our best ideological tag. It is about delivering meaningful and sustainable livelihoods for everybody, giving priority to the disadvantaged.

Greens would simplify the tax system. Income tax would remain as the main form of direct governmental taxation but would only kick in above a minimum level. That minimum would be set by a Green government as the amount required to meet an individual's basic needs, made to substitute and supplement personal tax-free allowances, and paid to every citizen as a matter of right. Greens call this a 'Citizen's Income', described in the Manifesto for the Sustainable Society: 'A Citizen's Income is an unconditional,

non-withdrawable income payable to each individual as a right
of citizenship. It will not be subject to means testing and there
will be no requirement to be either working or actively seeking
work.' (EC 730).

There is a clear principle at play. Everybody, in a civilised
society, is entitled to have their basic needs met so there should
be no strings attached to the allowance that guarantees provision.
This provision will be contributed to by everybody earning above a
certain amount, collectively, and serve as a safety net for everybody,
taken individually. There is no linkage between receipt of the
Citizen's Income and the expectation to find work, but this does not
mean that people will not want to work or that we would become a
society of layabouts.

Work will be recognised for the good that it is. Working
conditions and labour itself will be meaningful, not drudgery. Not all
work is paid, and the Citizen's Income will enable people to pursue a
greater range of opportunities, including voluntary work. The MfSS
says, 'The Green Party recognises that work plays a central part in
a healthy and balanced life. People have a natural desire to make a
contribution to the common good. We therefore oppose the view
of work which treats it as an unfortunate necessity to be performed
by machines whenever possible and we oppose the reduction of
people's working lives to a series of simple, repetitive activities.'
(PB 460–61) Jean Lambert, our Green MEP for London, has been
instrumental in getting the EU Working Time Directive introduced
to the UK as a way of protecting against unfair conditions at work.

On earnings over and above the guaranteed Citizen's Income,
rates of income tax would be set according to the principle that
those on higher incomes will pay higher marginal rates of tax.
Rates higher than 40 per cent would be introduced for those on
the highest incomes. For Greens, it is a mistake to think that well-
being can be measured in purely economic terms, but nor is it true

that the product of human labour is its sole factor. We correct the misapprehension that well-being and money are equivalent and the redistribution of taxable earnings on grounds of fairness and just deserts for all can be better understood.

Greens would also reform inheritance tax, whilst retaining its principle purpose as a means 'to reverse and prevent the accumulation of wealth and power by a privileged class' (MfSS, EC750). Tax due on an inherited estate will be calculated with proper regard to the circumstances of the recipient as well as the donor, i.e. on a 'recipient basis', and gifts made during a donor's lifetime would be assessed, too. This would result in a more equitable 'accessions' tax system.

Transport

A hallmark of a Green society is the maintenance of a civic society and public service ethos *worthy of the name*. For thirty years, Labour and Conservative governments have pursued an unrelenting stripping of the public assets and public services in the name of economic goals and a misguided ideological bias towards the private sector. Greens would put the public back into public services and goods. It is difficult to overstate the damage that has been done to the quality of public services – and, in turn, to the quality of lives of all those who depend upon such services – over this period.

Consider the fragmentation of the railways. Passengers get hit with above-inflation fares increases, and are being priced off the railways and tempted on to low cost airlines for inland destinations. Fares information is difficult to decipher and often one needs to know what one is looking for in order to find it. The fare on offer can also be affected by how one accesses the information. When I ask a cashier for the cheapest fare for a regional destination she asks what time I am travelling. But that depends on the fare, so we are stuck in a Catch-22 of the cashier not being able to tell me the cheapest fare because she needs the time, but I cannot give her a time because I need the cheapest fare.

Even when the national rail watchdog has imposed a freeze on peak fares for train operating companies passengers still face the possibility of a shifting deadline of what counts as an off-peak journey; as a way for the train companies to circumvent the watchdog. Did I say 'passengers'? We get called 'customers' because we only get treated as a collective commodity.

When things go wrong, such as in extreme weather, one of the main deficiencies is lack of public information. Nobody seems to take responsibility for telling us what is going on, perhaps for fear of missing a reliability target that would impact upon the subsidies received by an operating company, or result in a fine. But this treats passengers as *secondary* to the transport system that is meant to carry them; now run as a business for profit, not a service that employees and users can feel proud of. Even on its own terms, if there was proper competition, access to information about delays or cancellations would allow passengers to consider alternatives. Alas, for most train routes, the inconvenience of disruption cannot be alleviated by some like-for-like alternative. But at least passengers would know enough to be able to proceed with least worst alternatives.

Greens would return the railways into public ownership and invest enough for a reliable and convenient service. Fares would be simplified, transparent and proportional to actual cost, including the environmental cost. Instead of people feeling compelled to use the private car for many journeys, as now, the public alternative would be so affordable and attractive that the car would become the exception, not the norm.

It is difficult to overstate the negative impact of the car on everyday life. Road traffic is one of the major sources of environmental pollutants, such as carbon monoxide, carcinogens, noise and CO_2 itself. Car ownership has reached such a level that residential parking is a growing problem, encroaching on the public space to the extent that walking, cycling and other human-scale transport modes have become more difficult.

Greens would reverse this trend by investing in a hierarchy of transport modes, with walking and cycling at the top, followed by train, light rail and bus corridors; and by reducing reliance on private cars, heavy goods vehicles and aeroplanes. Road traffic accidents are the biggest cause of unnatural death in the UK. Greens would promote car-free housing developments and car club schemes, which both result in a significant reduction in overall cars – parked or in transit.

Rather than trains being run for the benefit of the companies and their shareholders, they would be run for the sake of moving passengers comfortably, reliably and cheaply. Passengers should not have to queue for ticket purchases, or ticket collection, or have to compete for seats or standing room, or have to fork out small fortunes for season tickets.

On the buses, the practice of turning out a bus full of passengers in order to 'regulate' the service should be a last resort. A bus which is full, other things being equal, has been deployed to maximum effect; and people should be able to rely upon their expectation that it will continue to its advertised destination. The idea that one can minimise future disruption by inconveniencing actual passengers is a highly questionable practice. Greens would work to ensure that bus services were frequent and the public transport network was integrated so people could move seamlessly between different forms of transport; more cycle hubs at train stations would help.

Public services should be fit for public use, which means excellent, not sub-standard. The benefits for the passenger are obvious. Instead of passengers arriving late, feeling frustrated and cheated, journeys would run to time, leaving people satisfied and grateful to live here.

Postal services

Greens believe trade unions have a major role to play in re-establishing the public services and reviving their faltering standards. The idea of a public service ethos is friendly to unions but not to franchises set up to exploit government sales of public assets and services; a move begun by Thatcher and accelerated under Blair.

We recognise the vital role that well-managed, democratic unions have historically played, and will continue to play, in delivering quality public services and protecting the rights and enhancing the working conditions of the labour force. In the preamble to the Trade Unions section of the MfSS, Greens proclaim their support for 'the right of working people to form and join free democratic and self-governing trade unions, without restriction by employer or government. [We] share the unions' belief in working together to give individuals more say in their own lives. Unions should be participatory democracies, encouraging active involvement of all the workers they represent.' (WR400)

The expertise of ordinary workers is indispensable to the proper functioning of a service and their dedication and loyalty helps maintain standards. It is not the implementation of an internal market – with its proliferation of incentives, in whatever sector – that contributes either to job satisfaction or, in turn, to high quality labour. Rather, it is a sense of *common ownership* in the well-being of the state-run services, on behalf of both providers and users, that contributes to high standards.

What would inspire you more to do your job well? The thought that by meeting a sales target, you stood a better chance of receiving a performance-related bonus? Or because the recipient of the service was genuinely delighted and would come back for more? The former is a quantitative measure of success; but the latter qualitative.

Everybody wins when we act to pursue public goods for

the good of the public, instead of for our own benefit. Trying to promote a public good for private gain is a kind of category mistake. Such mistakes have been encouraged and facilitated by past successive governments, determined to pursue the ideological fantasy of continued economic growth for its own sake.

What gives the lie to the half-baked notion that you should have to pay the going rate in order to recruit and retain the best staff, in whatever environment, is that the best paid have often shown themselves to be the least capable, on performance-related terms. Rather, the best staff are often worst paid, upon whose shoulders the reputation of the service once lay and is now being squandered by executive directors who lack the competency for the role. Gross banking mistakes were made by highly paid bosses that helped to precipitate the financial crisis, without the need for relevant qualifications.

Consider Royal Mail. What's the price of a first or second class stamp? For a given weight and delivery time, what's the price difference? How do you tell a small letter from a large letter or small packet? Our once first class service has suffered from short-termist ideological thinking and a compulsion to increase customer options. It would cost the Royal Mail more to deliver your letter to a remote Scottish Isle than to a neighbouring suburb, but subsidy by the majority on behalf of a minority is part of an unwritten social contract. The contract says that although you might only occasionally want to make use of a long-distance destination, we are quite prepared to subsidise you if you occasionally subsidise us. We would rather enjoy a service that facilitates this, as one letter amongst others, and insures any one of us against prohibitive expense.

The path of a letter is highly varied, but the service would have them treated equally for purposes of cost. Such equality is what *defines* a public service. Taking advantage of economies of scale, subsidies of the few by the many remind us that we are part of the larger whole. The whole is nothing less than a society and the value we seek to give it. Although the principle of a same-priced stamp for anywhere in the country has not yet been destroyed, it has been undermined by the proliferation of pricing bands based on size, in addition to weight.

A negative impact of more price bands is the inconvenience of not knowing how much postage to prepare for an item without a special visit to the post office; and invariably the need to queue. Frustration and misinformation can result, depending on how you ask. In a comparison of postage quoted online with that from an office, it transpired I would have been undercharged by the website, since it had not distinguished between a letter and a small packet. Mispayment could have meant a penalty to the recipient, or even non-delivery. The lack of simple price bands frustrates the user in finding the cheapest way of preparing an item for the post. Perhaps that was the intention, to maximise revenue by increasing the ways of being charged?

Unlike the previous regime – under which price rises and changes were less frequent so one could actually keep track of them – the current methods treat the user as a consumer of products. What any user would rather have is a reliable, cheap service. Notwithstanding the challenges faced by the postal service because of the increased use of other media, one does not achieve sustainability by abandoning the qualities that made the service attractive at all.

Public services

Before reviewing the Green Party stance on health and housing, here is an illustration of how customer service can go wrong. When I thanked a call centre employee for resolving a query on my utility bill, it did spoil the effect when he then wanted to pass me on to his supervisor – *so that the gratitude could be documented.*

I obliged, but felt that the thanks had been cheapened, for being repeated upon request. Gratitude is often spontaneous, and the formal recording of it – as if a questionnaire was being completed – can be quite inappropriate. The billing problem was correctly resolved, and arguably without any special credit due to the employee – not beyond the call of duty. I was simply grateful that he had taken my word for it that the original bill, for whatever reason, had arrived after the deadline for receipt of a prompt payment discount – making it impossible for anybody to settle it on time. Raising the matter upon discovery of an extra charge on the next quarterly bill, I was appreciative that he didn't seek to question my account. Maybe he had noticed a habit of prompt payment; no matter. More important was his ability to *trust me* and to be able to spot the difference between somebody who was pretending and somebody who was not. The amount was small, but the spirit of the practice of prompt payment, and any discount accruing from it was not so small.

Gratitude can have an effect beyond its original expression, by contributing to job satisfaction for the employee or helping to foster good relations with users. That helps to create a good working ethos, in which user and employee are treated as ends in themselves, not solely means to each others' ends; even when they don't know each other.

Recording gratitude does not provide best evidence of a good worker, when really that should be apparent in other ways – like body language showing somebody to be good at their job and facilitating a service *for its own sake*. With the prospect of job insecurity, perhaps it is forgivable that the employee would wish to have their good offices noted by their supervisor. But that would be to alter the purpose of the thanks, which was *intrinsic not instrumental*.

Health

In healthcare, the recording of user satisfaction is just one symptom of the shift away from a public service ethos to a market driven one – with a subsequent proliferation of patient targets and hospital league tables. Unfortunately, even when a region's share of the national health budget has seen a significant increase, the administrative burden caused by the shift has been paid for in ways which leave vital services more vulnerable. Recall the woman who confronted Blair on his hospital walkabout. Perhaps it was unfair for her to put Blair on the spot like that, since no Prime Minister can take personal charge over each and every medical resourcing decision that gets made up and down the country.

However, a PM, and his health minister, can be held to account for promoting and enacting free market reform that goes on to have a detrimental effect on the morale of a national health service, especially when such reform was forced through against the better wisdom of health practitioners. A PM can be held morally to account for having a negative impact on the context in which medical decisions are made after enacting bad policy decisions nationally. Perhaps that is why, in unconscious recognition of the fact, Blair was immediately speechless.

Greens will continue to defend, and take every step to restore, an NHS that is publicly owned and free to all at the point of use. We see access to healthcare as a basic human right, not a commodity to be bought or sold. We are opposed to the private finance initiative, which only leads to loss of public accountability and increase in public debt – all of which result in an uneven service and threaten the quality of local hospitals. Greens are committed to restoring free prescriptions, such as for eye tests and dental treatment, and better access to contraception and family planning services. We aim to establish a much firmer basis for preventative medicine, as part of a long-term strategic and holistic goal for health provision for

all. By encouraging a lower carbon lifestyle, individuals who grow
and eat their own locally sourced vegetables, or adopt human scale
transport, will automatically improve their health and quality of life.
We are not opposed to the emergence of polyclinics – community
health centres, able to provide some care traditionally provided
in hospitals but closer to home – so long as they are made to
complement pre-existing local services rather than to replace them.

The BMA manifesto for the 2010 general election is wholly
consonant with Green Party health policy: 'Health care services
need to be based on cooperation rather than competition. Doctors
are concerned that uncontrolled competition, plurality and
market-based reforms will result in greater fragmentation of care
that will ultimately reduce the standard and quality of care that
patients receive.'

Housing

Housing is another of the basic provisions of a just society, to
which all persons are entitled as of right. Unfortunately, the
current housing crisis is a result of Labour's failure to replace the
1.5 million homes that were sold through the Thatcherite right-to-
buy legislation as part of the housing stock of local authorities.
The Green Party would restore funding for sustainable new
housing stock, enable empty properties to be brought back into
use, through retrofitting as necessary, and defend public ownership
under the control of local authority elected representatives as part
of mixed provision for social housing. New stock would contain
at least 60 per cent affordable housing and targets would be set to
address homelessness urgently.

In 2009, the Greens unveiled a progressive new policy for
the housing sector – aptly named 'right to rent' instead of right
to buy – to ensure that private homeowners were protected from
repossession or eviction. Thus: 'home owners who are unable to

meet their mortgage payments and are under threat of repossession would have a right to transfer ownership to the council, at less than market value, in exchange for the right to remain in the home and pay rent as council tenants'. (HO411) The cost to the councils would be met by government grants or public bonds.

There's something rather dispiriting about the idea that people should only seek to do a good day's work because they had some personal gain to be independently got from it. Many of us spend much of our adult lives in employment, and some of us are fortunate enough to do something we enjoy. The extent to which we do enjoy our work is directly affected by the value of the goods or services we contribute towards, and the opportunity we are given to make a difference, in whatever role.

By enabling us to focus on a greater collection of public and environmental priorities and goals, a Green government would increase the rewards of work and the numbers likely to benefit from job satisfaction. By challenging *false hierarchy*, in public institutions and in the wider society, and replacing it with egalitarian structures, a Green government would increase social mobility. We will replace hierarchic stasis and entrenchment with equality and motion.

Education

The Green Party would advance an integrated, all-inclusive, essentially public-funded approach to learning and education, with significant reforming legislation where necessary.

The main flaws of the current educational system are as follows: (1) an over-reliance on tests for school-age children – Greens would abolish SATs; (2) an over-reliance on quantitative school league tables, which take vital staff resources away from actual teaching – Greens would abolish such tables, and maintain and improve Ofsted inspections with a school self-assessment element; (3) infiltration of the core curriculum with vested interests from private sponsors, facilitated by prior government legislation – Greens are opposed to City Academies and Trust schools on such grounds, and would require greater community participation in their management (where such schools already exist) and stop more from being built; (4) an emphasis on artificial targets in higher education, such as 50 per cent post-school entrants, which bear no relation to either student need, at a given stage in life, or the collective interests of the society – Greens would put greater emphasis on *lifelong learning*, recognising the role of the workplace and less formal approaches, in addition, for invaluable training and education.

We would properly fund higher education to enable people to study more flexibly and at a time better suited to their interest and desire. Student tuition fees would be abolished for all but overseas applicants, whose fees have been artificially raised due to a lack of proper public funding. The higher education sector has used overseas students to try to bridge this funding gap; thereby impacting unfairly on students from both home and abroad who were better qualified than their richer counterparts.

An elaboration of key elements of Green educational policy is in order.

Firstly, we do not accept that students should be made to specialise in various subject areas too soon, sometimes as young as ten, as would be required by specialist schools either currently co-funded by the government, or run by some private or faith-based schools. Greens would ensure that all children were entitled to be educated locally at a comprehensive school – to the highest standard – with admissions criteria set by the local authority in conjunction with the local community, who would gain representation on the schools' governing boards. The idea of comprehensive education is ably expressed in the MfSS: 'School leaving qualifications will encourage a broad curriculum that gives equal value to academic, vocational, creative and practical subjects.' (ED059) We also believe that the best environment for school education is a mixed-ability one, where overall standards have been shown to be higher, and that would encourage social cohesion.

Whilst it is expected that most parents or guardians would wish to send their children to a well-regarded, properly state-funded local community school between the ages of seven and sixteen, there would not be an obligation to do so. A guardian would be entitled to educate their child in another environment – such as the home – if they were able to work in partnership with the local authority in meeting the core needs of the educational curriculum.

Lifelong learning

The wider philosophy underpinning the Greens' education policy is the value of lifelong learning and the belief that such learning can productively take place in a variety of formal and informal contexts. Education has the potential to impact upon the whole outlook and behaviour of an individual – by imparting skills, or bringing to life innate capacities, or teaching critical reflection upon deeply held convictions – so it can exercise and emancipate in equal measure. Green education is the exact opposite of that Blairism, 'The more you learn the more you earn.' It is a subversion of the educational impulse – and a cynical misrepresentation of its purpose – to suppose that knowledge can be reduced to money in the bank. Of course, Blair meant that by aspiring to become better qualified, his model citizen could then increase his employment opportunities or advance his career. Perhaps that is not an ignoble ambition, but it should not be made the primary end of education, or so represented.

No, put simply, *the more you learn the more you learn*. Greens believe in the value of education for its own sake: 'Adult education should embrace and encourage learning for learning's sake and as such funding for additional courses will be decided at a local level, without it having to be target driven and focused only on qualifications.' (MfSS, ED265)

It is to seriously downgrade the value of education, and its place in wider society, to limit or prioritise its state sponsorship to meet the end of career-focused qualifications. This reduction is again betrayed by the policy phrase 'knowledge economy'. The most charitable interpretation of this idea is that knowledge and skills are instrumental as currency in the modern world; that to be qualified is to have expertise that can be traded as a commodity might be. Hence the so-called knowledge economy is both an analogy with trade and an identification with trade. But the problem with the notion is that it diminishes the role of education to its cash value in the workplace, literally and figuratively, and squeezes out the intrinsic value associated with knowledge. To be educated, in the broadest sense, is to have a wherewithal about the world. Formal qualifications are neither necessary nor sufficient to that end. Not all academic philosophers are philosophers and not all philosophers are academics.

Higher education

The instrumental attitude to education is increasingly evident in this government's approach to funding in higher education. The government's announcement that it intends to cut funding to the universities by asking them to shorten degree courses, from three to two years, betrays instrumentalism – without, that is, proper regard to the negative impact this would have on quality.

In recent years, a differential course fees structure has been imposed by the government that penalises students who may wish to enrol on a course for a Qualification that is Equivalent or Lower (hence government jargon 'ELQ') than one they already have. They will now have to pay more to learn more. This clearly replaces the ethos of learning for its own sake with one in which you are discouraged from further study, if and when you already have a qualification equivalent to or higher than your intended further course of study. Nor does the restriction pay any attention to the fact that the intended qualification will invariably lie in a subject different to that in which the student will already have an equivalent or higher qualification. Such a disincentive is not even rational on the government's own terms – to enable people to access education for the purpose of reskilling. It is not as though students will be seeking to duplicate their prior qualifications – at the same level, in the same subject area.

No, this is another cynical educational policy that would rather have it as a consequence that *the less you earn the more you would have to pay to learn.*

Religion in schools

Green policy on faith-based schools was updated at the national party conference in 2009. The section contains an affirmation that religious diversity should be respected, but not at all costs, thus: 'Education should include a . . . recognition of religious and cultural diversity [but] encourage critical engagement with, and non-dogmatic exposure to, diverse, sometimes competing, worldviews and beliefs – whether based on culture, religion or spirituality.' (MfSS, ED170) In this, the Greens recognise that not all religious teachings are equally consonant, either when comparing different religions, or with every aspect of a liberal educational framework. Greens go on to affirm that 'religious instruction, as distinct from religious education in understanding different religions may only take place outside of school curriculum time; no publicly funded school shall be run by a religious organisation; and, privately funded schools run by religious organisations must reflect the inclusive nature of British society and become part of the Local authority admissions system.' (MfSS, ED175–7, excerpted)

This shows a clear attempt to mark a division between an educational environment which promotes understanding and would encourage critical reflection, now and into the future, and one in which beliefs were communicated in such a way as to indoctrinate. It is clear that not all sets of beliefs are subject to this kind of division. For example, we would not ordinarily describe teaching about the geometry of the earth as subject to caution about dogmatising. We take it that such facts as we have about the earth are verifiable and worth imparting to students coming to the topic for the first time. However, with beliefs conditioned by faith, or subject to contested interpretations of historical episodes, we are right to want to guard against the over-exposure of a youngster to any one contested religious world-view as though it were fact. The Green policy does not outlaw such instruction, but it would police it within the state-funded classroom – with the aim of curtailing aggressive religious indoctrination by teaching about all religions in a comparative way. From the other direction, Greens would ensure quality control of the admissions policies of any faith school – when operating outside the state-funded system – by insisting they were to engage with the local authority in admissions processes.

Bad faith and moderation

Unfortunately, this kind of protection against discrimination by a faith school in its admissions policy has already been required under the law. In 2009, the Supreme Court ruled that the refusal by the Jewish Free School in Kenton to admit a boy because it did not recognise his mother as Jewish amounted to racial discrimination, in the legal sense of the term. Although the boy's father was Jewish by birth, his mother had converted at a synagogue not recognised by Orthodox Judaism – or at least not recognised by the school in its interpretation of what its admissions policy required.

Dr Simon Hochhauser, United Synagogue President, responded

to the ruling: 'The United Synagogue is extremely disappointed with the Supreme Court ruling which interferes with the Torah-based imperative on us to educate Jewish children, regardless of their background'. This is a defiant response which puts his interpretation of what a religious text requires of him before an interpretation of human rights legislation, and what that would require of a school's admissions policy to ensure that racial discrimination was not being perpetrated. Dr Hochhauser's statement betrays a failure to distinguish between what the Torah says, his interpretation of what is said therein, and what the Torah commands of him with respect to the school's admissions policy.

It is arguable that the type of discrimination effected by the school's admissions policy was based more on a determination of religion than of race – especially in light of the explanation given for excluding the boy based on the religious credentials of the mother and the school's claim to want to revise its selection process after the ruling. However, it is not clear that this could constitute any kind of moral defence of the practice, given the human rights imperative to not discriminate on grounds of religion either. It would certainly be hard to credibly claim that whilst the school may not have sought to discriminate on racial grounds it did not seek to discriminate on religious grounds either. Dr Hochhauser's qualification, 'regardless of their background' appears to be made to insulate the school against the accusation that they were somehow applying a race-based principle of exclusion. However that may be, the policy clearly had the effect of excluding a boy, whose family believed they had every entitlement to seek and be granted admission to the school. Whether the boy was excluded *tout court*, on religious or racial grounds, or given a lower priority on such grounds, he was still discriminated against for reasons that could not be defended on human rights grounds. He was denied equal access to a school for an allegedly arbitrary reason. His parents had a reason to resent this, and did indeed resent it. Under Green Party educational policy, however, faith schools' admissions would be overseen by the local authority – not somebody's putative interpretation, or claimed knowledge, of divine authority.

Greens would seek to create a learning environment which left sufficient intellectual and emotional space for children to be able to critically inspect the claims of religious interpreters – and to be able to reject them, as adults – especially where those claims would appear to be both dogmatic and contrary to the letter, and indeed spirit, of human rights legislation. The importance of this cannot be overstated. Otherwise children may have beliefs impressed upon them without sufficient regard to the factual or intellectual basis for those claims; nor could they be expected, at such an age, to have developed the critical capacities to challenge them. They need to be safeguarded from the possible dangers of religious indoctrination.

Interpretation of what Judaism might require of a faith-based school's admission policy is not the only arena in which a religion, or a bad interpretation of it, might contravene the liberal values of a society. A spokesperson for Islam4UK – an extremist Islamist organisation proscribed by the government – has described their vision for a country bound by Sharia law. Such a regime would be wholly incompatible with the man-made laws of this country; indeed that is their want. However, there are clear, probably stronger, grounds to want to have such ideology openly challenged, if not subjected to ridicule, so long as they do not incite murder or racial hatred.

Since we have here, in the UK, at least two different groups pronouncing upon what God would command of them, but would make claims that are incompatible with one another, they cannot both be right in their claims to know what God commands. If there is a God, he cannot command that we would follow a set of propositions that are mutually inconsistent with one another.

Greens do not purport to know what God commands, or

even whether there is a god, but they do purport to know that it is better for all members of society – for all their diverse opinions, however deeply held – to be able to get along as one amongst equals. They would be encouraged in that civic attitude, or at least not impeded from it at any early age, when taught alongside one another – whatever their background or putative religion. The education section of the MfSS reinforces this: 'It is important to preserve both diversity of opportunity and equality of opportunity for students (of all ages) in an education system which encourages social cohesion.' (ED004) This is to demonstrate our belief in a society of equals through action.

We should not be propagating the idea that the circumstances into which a child is born – in particular, the religious predilections of their parents – should somehow determine who they may or may not mix with at school. Introducing, and applying, such a discriminatory idea in the mind of a child will not help them to integrate into society as one amongst equals. Such an idea might even foster prejudice about a child, who having been excluded from a school might then feel somehow inferior or less important. Greens take a stand against, and fight to combat, such prejudice in the wider society; so it is only consistent that they should seek to legislate against exclusion in the classroom. Greens are nothing if not holistic in politics.

The membership of the Green Party is diverse with respect to religious belief or none. We are a broad church in that regard. Moreover, we do not have any mechanism for soliciting data on the religious predilection or none of individual members and probably have no desire to do so. The majority of the general population, with religious belief or none, are moderate in their espousal or practice of theism, agnosticism or atheism. They are moderate by definition, as they have no desire to overturn man-made laws on the pretext that they were not ordained by their god and do not conform to their claimed knowledge of God's command. Of course, a responsible citizen may seek to have oppressive laws abolished or reformed, as do members of the Green Party, but not because, at bottom, God commands it; rather because we think it would be morally right to do so.

Whether or not, as individuals, we seek to *validate* our claims to know right or wrong by way of God's will, ultimately, we are still responsible for choosing to believe as we do, and as such are accountable for those beliefs. Make no mistake, we do have a choice in our adoption of a controversial reading of a religious text that would have oppressive or perverse consequences. Alternatively, we could choose to adopt a moral outlook – based on religious interpretation or none – worthy of the unconditional recognition of the value of every human being as one amongst equals.

An enlightened outlook also would realise our collective responsibility to look after the planet for the sake of future generations and the other species we share it with.

Equality and sexual orientation

One of the most difficult balances to be struck in politics is knowing how to adjudicate rival or competing claims for finite resources or recognition. The Green Party believes that we don't just have entitlements to things, but that we have duties towards others, too. Enjoyment of rights implies *exercise of responsibilities*, both for its own sake and to ensure that consideration is to be given to us when we are ever in need or in trouble. In the statement of principles to the Rights and Responsibility chapter of the MfSS, Greens identify 'human responsibilities, not as a counterbalance to individual and collective rights, but as integral with them', because of 'the interconnectedness of all things, the finiteness of resources and the ethical imperative in politics'. (RR200)

I have already elaborated on the justification for the Greens' position on the state funding of faith schools – *we would not fund them*. We seek to facilitate social cohesion and think that this is best achieved by funding all-inclusive, local comprehensive schools that neither used proclaimed religion as a criterion for selection nor sought to promote any one religion over and above another in the schools. In this, there is a clear commitment to a liberal rights framework in which human rights take centre stage and actions which would undermine those liberties, or risk compromising them – whether or not motivated by cultural or religious interpretations or misinterpretations – would need to be checked or curtailed.

The focus on religion is a good place to start when considering what latitude is to be given, in a society which prides itself on being free, to the expression of diverse opinions amongst the general population. Religiously inspired actions, as proclaimed by their agents, are sometimes condemned as illegitimate, and for good reason. Since there are no circumstances in which the terrorist attacks on the Twin Towers on 9/11 could be justified, cutting short the lives of 3,000 unwitting individuals, then there are no circumstances in which they could be justified on self-proclaimed religious grounds either. Since there are no circumstances in which the attacks on London civilians in July 2005 could be justified, then they could not be justified by recourse to a perverted interpretation of Islam either.

We should take care to distinguish between the *self-proclaimed* religious ideologies of terrorist bombers – and what actions they would take their fanaticism to justify – and the rational or sensible interpretation of religious texts and traditions. That is not to say that any one religion could not defy rational or sensible interpretation in every respect; for sure, disagreement about figurative or literal meaning has given rise to a variety of outlooks even within the same religion; and sometimes there appears to be more commonality between individuals who proclaim to be from different religions than between those who claim to be from the same.

Commitment to a human rights framework gives us the moral standpoint to be able to make sense of transgressions to basic standards of human decency, such as the denial or extinction of another's right to life, without undue attention to the self-proclaimed reasons given for those transgressions. *Actions speak louder than words* in this arena, including identification of the right description under which a heinous action should be understood for what it is ahead of the self-justifying proclamations of their perpetrators, with whatever perverted ideological baggage they might carry. We do not necessarily take the perpetrator's word for it that his self-justifying account is the correct moral account of the action. This can apply equally to self-justifying accounts of leaders who wage war on foreign peoples, about which we will have more to say later. Might is not necessarily right.

Homophobia

Unfortunately, immoderate, or even half-literal interpretations of religious texts give citizens concerned about human rights and anti-discrimination plenty to campaign about. In January 2006, Sir Iqbal Sacranie, leader of the Muslim Council of Britain, was asked on BBC radio, in the context of a discussion about same-sex civil partnerships, whether he believed homosexuality was harmful to society. He answered, 'Certainly it is a practice that – in terms of health, in terms of the moral issues that comes along in society – it is not acceptable. And what is not acceptable, there is a good reason for it. Each of our faiths tells us that it is harmful and I think, if you look into the scientific evidence that has been available in terms of the forms of various other illnesses and diseases that are there, surely it points out that where homosexuality is practised there is a greater concern in that area.'

Justifiable outrage was directed at the BBC from offended listeners for their broadcast of this comment about Sacranie's attempt to find a scientific basis for his offensive views. My own comment was posted to the BBC website: 'Sir Iqbal's attitudes on homosexuality will have struck many heterosexuals as sadly those of a bigot and not fit for the twenty-first century. What that says about organised religion in the twenty-first century is an even bigger question.'

I am proud to say that such offence is also shared by my party, which couches equality of sexual orientation in the following terms: 'Attempts to enforce heterosexuality are as much a violation of human rights as racism and sexism, and must be challenged with equal determination[.] Young people have the right to be brought up to understand that they may experience homosexual or heterosexual feelings or both, and that either or both are to be welcomed as having potential to enrich their lives and those of the people around them.' (MfSS: RR500, RR502)

The reason I expressed my own disgust from the point of view of a heterosexual was the desire to demonstrate a wider point about human rights. Prejudice against gays offends against gay and straight, *as human beings alike*. To make the accusation from the point of view of a heterosexual potentially strengthens the claim of group solidarity and human kinship by showing that you do not have to be gay to be affected by prejudice against gays. Indeed, we would be failing in our duties as human beings to think otherwise. One does not speak out and campaign against prejudice only because one is materially affected or directly implicated as the target of that prejudice. Rather, one demonstrates a commitment to equality irrespective of whether one is or is not the target of that prejudice. For sure, since the injustice of prejudice is often exacerbated by the fact that the targeted group is also in a minority, it is of paramount importance that everybody take collective responsibility for combating the injustices suffered by the few.

It is possible that Sacranie's self-proclaimed faith-based prejudice against gays is also grounded in cultural difference. But religious beliefs and differences are often promulgated through different cultural backgrounds and the Green Party seeks to affirm the priority of human rights when conflicts with those rights would otherwise arise: 'Accepting the universal dimension to the concept of human rights requires recognition of the cultural dimension, in that different cultures do not always share the same view of what constitutes a good life. But the Green concept of responsibilities as an integral part of rights transcends such possibly conflicting views.' (MfSS, RR202)

Any attempt to justify homophobia or other prejudice on the basis of cultural difference is rightly illegitimate under this framework. This is commonly expressed, within the liberal framework, as the requirement, even obligation, *not to tolerate the intolerable*. It is a misunderstanding of the liberal rights framework to suppose that diversity cannot be answerable, or made answerable, to a higher value against which it would otherwise sometimes offend.

Free speech and dirty hands

Although Sacranie, and spokespersons like him, do not always show themselves – or those they would seek to represent – in a good light, that does not mean that they cannot do, or have not done, good elsewhere – for example, in seeking to combat religious extremism (of other sorts) within their own communities. If we are to believe in the value of education, why should we not also allow that confronting a spokesperson with his own unwitting prejudice, in the process, could enable him to overcome that prejudice through needed self-examination which led to internal change of the right sort? Sartre once said *we should not judge a man a thief for eternity and deny him his ability to change.*

Perhaps Sacranie was entitled to express the views he sincerely held, in spite of others taking offence, and maybe there is advantage to be had in others recognising his prejudice for what it was and knowing how to judge him for it, or in attempting to make him answerable for it. Later in the same interview, Sacranie was quick to defend his own supposed entitlement to express his prejudices by appeal to tolerance and its place in society: 'Well, tolerance comes from both ways. We have an opportunity to express our views. This is what we have, this is the privilege we have living in an open democratic society. This is something which we felt deeply concerned about because we felt it [homosexuality] does not promote the social or family harmony in society . . . I have the right to express my view, others have the right to oppose and put their arguments.'

Sacranie makes tacit appeal to the value of free speech, but would misconstrue the preconditions for its proper exercise. Normally, in a topic such as the one in which Sacranie was asked for his controversial opinion, we would have rightly expected opportunity to be given for another to express a different view. Instead, disgruntled listeners felt they had to feed their objections through to the comments section of the station's website, but with no guarantee that their views, or views like them, would be posted to the site or read out by the broadcaster – either later in the programme or on a subsequent occasion. Whatever the failings of the man who articulated his prejudices on live radio, the broadcaster had also arguably failed in its responsibility to safeguard against prejudiced views going unchallenged. The topic was important enough, and line of questioning predictable enough, that the broadcaster should have insured against the possibility of offensive views going unchallenged at the time by having a more enlightened interviewee to hand, in addition.

Voltaire's maxim 'I may not like what you say, but I defend to the death your right to say it' is often quoted in the context of discussions about the entitlements and supposed infringements of free speech. This seems to be the same line of defence adopted by

Sacranie for himself; but both Voltaire and Sacranie fail to recognise that free speech is not, and never has been, absolute – and rightly so.

Firstly, *there is no such thing as free speech*, literally put. A precondition of the proper exercise of free speech, as in a debate, is due facilitation, in a manner which allows all parties the opportunity to have their views aired, according to their level of interest or state of knowledge. The goal of such facilitation is to have the topic of interest explored to such a degree that all sides may be satisfied that intellectual advance has been made. John Stuart Mill well understood the value of free speech, especially in the potential clash of truth with error, in the opportunity it gave all sides to have falsity exposed for what it was and to have truth strengthened, if not enlivened, through articulation and publicity. Therefore it is only by speakers exercising self-discipline, or via the enforcement of equal speaking rights, that the ends to which free speech properly aims at may be obtained. Thus, nobody is free to speak whenever they want or for as long as they would like, since that would adversely impact upon the liberty of others to exercise their own speech. Free speech has to be moderated to make sense, and so is not absolute as such, but conditional on the like exercise of others. The police do not ordinarily allow fascist marchers permission to chant outside a synagogue – and rightly so.

Thus understood and accepted, it is automatic that there is a time and a place for the exercise of speech, and other times and places when it may be accepted *by any reasonable observer* that speech of any sort is inappropriate or not wanted. A man who shouts 'FIRE!' as a prank in a cinema or auditorium, with the result that everybody evacuates has not served the ends to which the due exercise of speech was designed. Instead he could justifiably be blamed and held to account for acting in a manner that could be predicted to have caused maximum disruption, for no good reason.

Debates about the proper limits or otherwise of speech are

ubiquitous in politics and society, and for good reason. If we were to misunderstand, or simply did not get right, the preconditions of free speech, we could end up subverting the ends to which speech properly aimed.

Censorship and censuring

What entitlement, if any, did the leader of the BNP have to appear on BBC's *Question Time* debate as part of the political panel in October 2009? The programme would get aired with a delay, to insure against the broadcast of any unanticipated or unwelcome scenes. There was a great deal of public debate and controversy surrounding the BBC's inclusion of the BNP in its schedule. On the day, anti-fascist demonstrators amassed at the entrance to the BBC studios demanding that TV exposure be denied. A few hours ahead of the BNP leader's appearance on the programme, I was interviewed for the news. Opinions were probably as divided within the Green Party on this matter as they could have been in the country at large. On the one hand, there is the presumption that, other things being equal, groups or their representatives with something to say on a given topic will be given equal entitlement, including political parties. This certainly happens with respect to the entitlement, once certain electoral conditions have been met, of political parties to have a party election broadcast carried on the main channels in the run up to an election.

However, it is arguable that other things are not equal in a case such as *Question Time*. The BBC was setting a precedent by having the BNP on their programme for the first time, and whilst they did argue that a principle of impartiality required this of them, it is not clear that they were right to interpret it as an inviolable obligation. It did remain in their power to forego such an invitation.

Secondly, even after accepting that free speech does not entail an absolute entitlement to speak out of turn or at excessive length, nor does it allow that anything can be said within a properly facilitated debate. UK laws oblige the police to take full account of the risk of incitement to murder or racial hatred. If it could be shown that a speaker was intent on inciting racial hatred, then that would be sufficient to preclude them from the enjoyment of speaking rights. A correlation could also be highlighted between the appearance of a far-right ideologue on television and an increase in racially motivated attacks afterwards. However, one might have to take care in using such a putative correlation as justification for blocking a speaker; the existence of a causal relationship proves neither that the consequence was intended by the speaker nor that his appearance reliably explained subsequent aggressive behaviour. Contrariwise, a speaker may be found guilty of wilfully inciting racial hatred even if he does not succeed in that aim. *The intention is paramount*, including reasonable interpretations of that intention, quite independent of any speaker denials to the contrary. Still, the fact of a reliable correlation, with causal basis in past BNP public pronouncements, coupled with the desire to want to reduce the risk of harm to a vulnerable minority in society, should have been sufficient grounds to debar the BNP from inclusion on the panel.

I answered that the BBC was not obliged to give the BNP – 'a morally abhorrent' party political outfit – this sort of publicity, which would probably be to their advantage, and would put the nation at greater risk of subsequent harm than good. The BBC said they risked a legal challenge if they debarred the BNP from the programme; but they should have crossed that bridge if and when they came to it instead of conceding the BNP's case for them. The programme wasn't constitutionally set up to provide the BNP automatic access to the panel. Panellists were selected for a variety of reasons – often not transparent to the viewer – and in this case an invitation could have been foregone for a greater reason based in the risk of public harm, and with greater transparency than normal.

I added my voice to those amassed outside the BBC, calling for the BBC to revoke their invitation to the BNP at the eleventh hour, but also expressed my hope that – if the debate were to go ahead as planned – astute panellists would, where necessary, confront sinister or racist opinions.

The Green Party offers the view that debate is sometimes the best way to counteract offensive views. In a statement about how to manage invitations to platforms featuring controversial speakers, we say, 'Speakers and officers of the Green Party will only share platforms with groups who endorse racial, ethnic or national hatred at a public or private meeting where *that offers an opportunity to confront and oppose racism.*' (MfSS, RR804, italics added) It is understood that, where necessary or desirable, such opportunity will also be taken, not forgone. This still gives the option that a Green could share the platform but, for greater reason, choose not to take the opportunity to confront racism – *though opposed to racism* – because to do so would risk having the *agenda hijacked by the racist*, having the platform turned into something it was not meant to be, or giving the racist the publicity he craved. The potential for complexity of speech situations is probably too vast to be able to provide the party speaker with a hard-and-fast rule that was both unconditional and without exception.

The BBC panellists, and members of the audience, did a good job exposing and confronting offensive BNP attitudes and beliefs, but it is arguable that the BNP had the last laugh. If the BNP leader had managed to win some over, then he would have left with more than he started with. If he was made to look like public enemy number one – and the debate was certainly dominated by attacks upon him – then he might still have benefited from a perverse sort of sympathy vote. If and when censorship is no longer the best course of action – or not within our power to control – the consequences of the alternative action of *censuring* will need to be carefully considered, and self-restraint may also have its advantages as a damage limitation strategy.

Should Greens and other politicians seek to marginalise or engage with the BNP or other extremist organisations? When, for the first time in 2008, the BNP gained representation on the London Assembly, that will have shamed all right-thinking Londoners. But there is a case to answer those advocates of a strategy of marginalisation. If and when electoral politics delivers unpalatable results, are we not duty bound to share tables with politicians whose views we may rightly find abhorrent? What might otherwise become of such political arenas, if none of us were on guard to defend the rights of minorities against those who would seek to sow division and strife in our communities through perverted political means? Do we have such a low estimation of our ability to see truth and justice prevail over ignorance and prejudice? Is it not better to have the scale of the prejudice or hatred out in the open so that it can be openly confronted?

When the Green mayoral candidate Siân Berry left the City Hall stage after offering a vote of thanks on the night of the official declaration, nearly everybody both on and off stage followed – almost to cue – in anticipation that the BNP was going to be called next. I and a few remained, in order to hear the BNP candidate make a defiant address. We were right to turn our backs on him, for reasons of political solidarity and symbolism, but we were also right – some of us – to stay behind to mentally prepare for what might follow. To be forewarned is to be forearmed. Perhaps that is one of the strengths of an inclusive democracy, ugly results notwithstanding.

One might call this a kind of *dirtying of the hands* for the greater good, even to share an audience or a table with a racist advocate. Or do we rather suppose that Sartre was wrong in his belief that we should not judge a man a thief for eternity or deny them their ability to change? Perhaps we fear to look the BNP in the eye because we do not recognise them as human? Perhaps to do otherwise would be to recognise their capacity for reform, but we believe they are beyond reform? I do not profess to know the answer to those questions, but I think we should try to be consistent. How many of us would still rather shake the hand of ex-PM Blair, knowing that he was a key collaborator in the devastation meted upon Iraq, where so many innocents were killed? Do we really suppose that the lives of those innocent Iraqi children, life for life, were worth as much to Blair as if they had been Western European and predominately white? Doesn't this discrepancy make Blair as racist as the BNP, albeit covertly, and just as deserving of marginalisation? Are we at risk of using marginalisation as a means of expressing our indignation? Perhaps Blair is less open to reform than the BNP for thinking he is holy, but isn't he in denial about the true consequences of his actions? Yet maybe I could be reconciled to shaking Blair's hand if I knew that I could help save the life of just one Iraqi civilian. Perhaps we cannot afford the *moral luxury* of slighting his handshake, and the faraway innocents are secretly praying that we will engage. Perhaps the best we can do is *not to shake Blair's hand like we meant it*.

War and deception

Since the end of the Second World War, over sixty million people (predominately women and children) have been killed as a result of fighting, between states or within states, fighting done generally between men. It seems that, if anything, human civilisations are as determined as ever to resort to war to resolve conflicts about territory or resources or peoples' claims to self-determination on whose behalf they claim to be acting. Clausewitz, in *On War*, famously said that war is 'the continuation of policy by other means', and defined war as 'an act of violence intended to compel our opponent to fulfil our will [. . .] on an extensive scale'.

Unfortunately, in the last decade alone, our political leaders have been responsible for unleashing aerial bombardments upon unwitting civilian populations and mobilising offensive troops in foreign lands on the most discreditable of pretexts, with massive numbers of innocent people killed or maimed as a result. Not only have these innocents been mercilessly subjected to the *will* – in Clausewitz's terms – of a foreign aggressor, but they have been extinguished in the process. Bush and Blair will forever be associated, in the minds of a generation, as perpetrators of humanitarian outrages, for instigating and overseeing aggressive military operations in Afghanistan and Iraq. These leaders have yet to be brought to book and it is of paramount importance that they do not escape the full majesty – and indeed sobriety – of an international war crimes tribunal, answerable to the human rights canon so painstakingly drafted after the Second World War, as prefigured in the United Nations Charter and the Hague and Geneva conventions. Tens upon tens of thousands have literally suffered and died to no end, as if we are bound to continually repeat the mistakes of history by refusing to learn their lessons. Even after these moral outrages have been committed it is imperative that the international community – which showed itself so impotent to prevent them from occurring – pursue and criminally convict their key orchestrators and henchmen to restore some semblance of humanity to an international order which has been made considerably more dangerous as a result of their actions.

In this section, I will focus on the Green Party's moral and political reaction to the warring actions of the US and UK in Afghanistan and Iraq, and the illegitimate 'war on terror' rhetoric used to justify and frame those actions. Our reaction is that of any humane and rational person, or so I shall argue.

In a statement of principle, in the Green Party's Peace and Defence section of the MfSS, we say, 'Warfare in the context of present offensive weapon systems, nuclear or non-nuclear, is so dangerous that it cannot be regarded as a sane instrument of policy. Common security measures seek to build trust and cooperation, to prevent destructive conflict, to build a just local and global society based upon fairness.' (PD201) In Clausewitz's terms, this is to affirm that, if war is to be a means, then it must be a means of *last resort*, at best. Moreover, there are a whole series of conditions that would have to be explored, scrutinised and satisfied, were such resort to be even considered as the least worst of evils, with whatever subsequent outcomes. These conditions are often referred to as the *just war tradition* and it should be possible to plot most, if not all, theoretical positions towards the propensity to war, or its refrain, with respect to them. The stipulations of the just war tradition – based on the teachings of Aristotle, Cicero and Augustine – should be compulsory reading for any politician, and I shall attempt to summarise them.

Just war requirements

There are three parts to the just war methodology, and questions which need to be answered, which serve, respectively, (a) as a precaution against resorting to war on illicit grounds – *is going to war justified?*; (b) to dictate how a war may be waged more or less humanely, after defining moral limits – *what is allowed to happen in war?*; and (c) to oblige the victor to ensure that conditions are established which are conducive to restoring the infrastructure – *how are we going to leave things better after the war?*

States engaging in war, or aggressive actions, have been notoriously bad at ensuring that stability is reliably likely at the end of it, even if they achieved their warring aims. The recent operations in the Gulf were an example of this. What offended against even the likelihood that post-war aims could have been achieved is the justifiable accusation that war was not pursued by the US and UK, in these cases, with care for the civilian populations they purported to be trying to protect. To the contrary, whatever the stated aims and declared intentions, the result of the bombings was the death of tens of thousands of innocent people. If the war was waged for the benefit of the people bombed then it is a perverse way of showing it *to substantially kill a population in order to save them.* No – in reality, the warring aims were revealed in the priority that was given to the securing of oil fields by predominately US contractors, and betrayed in the contents of US neo-conservative ideological briefings headed 'Project for a New American Century', drafted prior to 9/11.

Whether Blair claims ignorance of the wider US ideological agenda, or even their economic motives, is not to his credit. Of further moral consequence was his determination to pursue those invasions, 'shoulder to shoulder', in spite of the unprecedented expert and public contestations to his stated reasons for taking the country to war. Those against the war were not only proven right in their suspicion of ulterior motives, but were right in their assessment of the falsity of the grounds given for going to war. Those stated grounds were focused, predominately but not exclusively, upon Saddam Hussein's putative capability to launch weapons of mass destruction – offensively, and possibly at the UK – within 'forty-five minutes'. Moreover, it is because Blair presided over the doctoring, and subsequent presentation to parliament and the UK public, of two intelligence briefings – upon which he staked his evidential case – that charitable motivation must be ruled out. He had deceived parliament and the public at large on the strength of his case. He remained *culpably ignorant*, at best, both of the true situation on the ground – as attested to by Hans Blix and other weapons inspectors – and of the motivations of the US administration; as was evident to any reasonable interpreter of international relations, who had warned against aggressive action, and as betrayed by the subsequent behaviour of the US.

It should come as no surprise, then, that according to the stipulations of the first clause of just war theory, the offensives on Afghanistan and Iraq are ruled out *tout court*. Those stipulations, in brief, are: (i) *just cause*, such as in self-defence; yet the UK was not facing an existential threat of any order, but was pursuing a pre-emptive attack (at best); (ii) the *right intention*; but the motive was predominately for securing oil, not saving peoples; (iii) the *right authority*; yet in this, UN resolution 1441 did not authorise 'all necessary means' nor had that been the intention of its signatories, and the shifty legal opinion produced by the Attorney General at the government's behest proved only that the law is far too important to be left to legal experts; (iv) *last resort*; clearly not, since weapons inspectors had been withdrawn, against their own will, but without Saddam expelling them; (v) *probability of success*; was arguably low, even though one of the aims to capture Saddam was achieved, against the odds; and (vi) *proportionality*; a grave transgression, given the methods used, since civilian casualties were disproportionate yet foreseeable.

The absence of this last condition was made more apparent in the manner in which the war was waged – *without due discrimination or humanity*. The scale of the civilian casualties which came about due to wholesale bombardment of densely populated areas could have been, and was, reliably predicted, given the methods used. This was in clear violation of the laws of war, in which non-combatant immunity must be protected.

The use of the term 'collateral damage', made current since the Gulf war of 1991, is particularly sinister. The attempt to categorise the deaths of innocent civilians as only so much 'collateral', is both morally abhorrent and intellectually repugnant. The perverse intellectual thought has it that what you do not primarily intend, although you might reliably bring it about and foresee it as a consequence, is no longer your moral responsibility. It were as though the fact that you did not *want* to kill masses of a civilian population – knowing they were on the receiving end of your blanket bombing, with nowhere else to flee – was sufficient to *beg off* on your moral responsibility for those deaths, whilst at the same time admitting that your actions did reliably, and would inevitably, cause those deaths. What gives the lie to the moral bankruptcy of this notion is that by far the primary outcome of such bombings was yet more civilian death and suffering. Therefore the deaths were disproportionate to any stated ends, however wished against. We do not ordinarily forgive a murderer for his crime simply because he pleads that he did not mean to pull the trigger or did not want to have to shoot the cashier in order to get his hand in the till.

Bush and Blair were guilty of more than wishful thinking, however. They were merciless in their bringing the heavens down upon unwitting innocents; and we should be unsparing of our application of human rights instruments in the aftermath by trying them for war crimes.

Harold Pinter's ferocious condemnation of Bush and Blair, in a speech to the anti-war crowds in 2003, was memorable: 'The United States is a MONSTER out of control! Run by a bunch of criminal lunatics! With Tony Blair as a hired, Christian thug!' Heady stuff. Heady times.

Since truth is one of the first casualties of war – assisted by properly briefed, embedded journalists – we should take care to call a thing by its proper name. Moral philosophers sometimes use the nomenclature 'double effect' to describe an effect that comes about as a secondary consequence of an action, that was not the primary intention as such. Health practitioners make use of the distinction to acquit themselves of the moral consequences of administering a heavy dose of diamorphine, with the intention of alleviating intolerable pain to a terminally ill patient, say – but in the knowledge that death may also be hastened as a result. The secondary outcome, if brought about intentionally, would not be consistent with the doctor's duty of care and his obligation to save lives – on most interpretations of the Hippocratic oath.

The attempt to classify 'collateral damage' as a sort of unintentional double effect cannot be sustained, however. There is no sense in which, from the population's point of view, they could will upon themselves the risk of certain harm from such bombardment – with the primary consequence not current pain relief, but infliction of pain or wanton death. If a political spin doctor should seek to play fast and loose with moral categories in this way, in an attempt to obfuscate the issue, we should know how to reply. Doctrine of double effect? Wrong. *Indoctrination of effective dissimulation?* Right.

The doctrine of collateral damage so called is simply an intellectually disreputable attempt by warmongers to conceal their culpability for civilian deaths which they have reliably brought about – to disguise it from themselves and from us. That is dissimulation, by no other name.

Iraq dossier

Just how audacious was the attempt by the UK and US to misrepresent the threat level from Iraq, in order to gain backing for a military response – or remove key obstacles to it? It mattered to the British public that an official briefing published by the government, and waved at by Colin Powell at the UN Security Council meeting of February 2003, purported to be based on classified material, but actually contained copied, unattributed sections from an Iraqi-American academic's PhD thesis. The discovery of the plagiarised content was made by a Cambridge academic – who subsequently alerted the media – about the dossier entitled, 'Iraq – Its Infrastructure of Concealment, Deception and Intimidation'.

To add to the offence of deliberate concealment by the UK about the true source of critical briefing matter – in an attempt to mislead us about the authoritativeness of its claims – the drafters also changed key words to suit their political ends. Changes to the plagiarised material were highlighted by Channel 4, and the reporter speculated on the obvious political motivation, 'to make for more sinister reading':

al-Marashi original		Downing Street (my italics)
'monitoring foreign embassies in Iraq'	⇨	'*spying* on foreign embassies in Iraq'
'aiding opposition groups in hostile regimes'	⇨	'*supporting terrorist organisations* in hostile regimes'

In a television interview, Blair betrayed his determination to press ahead with military action, disregarding the fact that most took absence of evidence of weapons of mass destruction as a reason against such extreme measures. Under sustained questioning, Blair retorted, 'Even if I'm the only person left saying it, I'm going to say it. I may be wrong in believing it, but I do believe it [.] I simply tell you, you can believe or don't believe it.' (BBC, 6 February 2003) Blair refused to counsel a shift in opinion based in factual appeal, or absence of evidence, even after redefining his problem to make the evidence easier to obtain – as, 'evidence of weapons of mass destruction programme-related activities'. It were as though Blair's beliefs needed to have no grounding in fact, or reckoning with absence of evidence. As a self-professed basis for taking a country to war this admission was both shocking and unforgiveable.

George Galloway brilliantly captured an insight about Blair's detachment from reality – and estrangement from himself – when he addressed one of the anti-war marches at the start of the invasion: 'You can see the GUILT written on his face!' Blair's unwitting display of conceit and denial, masquerading as strong leadership, was repeated in an answer of Alastair Campbell, responding as PMOS to accusations about doctoring and plagiarism: 'Our overall objective had been to give as full a picture as we could, not only of the Iraqi regime, but also of its deliberate policy of deception – without in any way compromising the intelligence sources on which the information was based.' (7 February 2003) This took doublespeak to new lows, as a means of countering the charge of deception, by charging another with deception.

Powell's assertions at a key UN meeting were also pure doublespeak: 'My colleagues, every statement I make today is backed up by sources, solid sources. These are not assertions. What we are giving you are facts and conclusions based on solid intelligence . . . I would call my colleagues' attention to the fine paper that the United Kingdom distributed yesterday which describes in exquisite detail Iraqi deception activities.' (Security Council, 5 February 2003) Powell relied upon such claims when he went on to say, 'war is a last resort; but it must be a resort.' However, the notion that a last resort is not a resort was never at issue, and it is sheer question-begging to suppose that such a resort had been reached. It had not, but this was yet another way, added to the deceptions about threat level, to create the illusion that key conditions of the just war doctrine had been met, although none of these could have been sufficient on their own, when correctly interpreted.

Given Powell's joint responsibility for the subsequent illegal use of force in Iraq, and responsibility for innocent dead, you can see I was justified in taking exception to his plan to visit my place of work.

State terror

Alas, more atrocities were committed under the command of George Bush, in which the UK was complicit, if not an active sponsor. Recall how the outrage of the 9/11 suicide attacks on New York and Washington was used as a pretext by the neo-conservative US administration not just to pursue disreputable ideological ends but to cast aside human rights protections that were enshrined in international law. The obscenity which was to become Guantánamo Bay, and the legal black hole into which its prisoners were 'extraordinarily rendered' as 'illegal combatants' – neither granted protections under the Geneva conventions nor as prisoners of war, but systematically kidnapped, exiled, interrogated, abused and tortured – came to symbolise the very depths of human cruelty, to which we thought, collectively, civilised beings could never return.

All this was happening in the twenty-first century, on the pretext of a 'war on terror' – a putative war on a subjective state of mind, a war that could be as unending as suited the illusionists' agenda. As advocates of a strong, internationally recognised human rights framework, the Green Party view was clear. Perpetrators of extreme acts of violence, designed to inflict maximum civilian casualties, or terrorise civilians, or wreak havoc in our cities, should not have their work done for them by our dismantling hard-won liberties ourselves. The perpetrators of those atrocities needed to be pursued single-mindedly, but through the courts, not outside of the law. Our position was well articulated in political statements, passed unanimously at successive conferences, including in 2002: '[We condemn] terrorism in all its forms, whether sponsored by states or individuals. Measures taken to combat terrorism must be carried out within the bounds of international law.' (RPD02.4)

Instead, religiously confused ideologues were made more powerful by having their status elevated in the eyes of the world, by the would-be oppressed state turned oppressor. We forewarned against such a course in 2001: 'The Green Party [believes] that violent countermeasures of any type would be a sure way of creating a hundred suicide bombers, willing to martyr themselves in protest.' (RPD01)

Cases of 'terrorism', if and when correctly described, should be consistently condemned, whoever the perpetrator. The term is unquestionably used as a term of moral disapprobation, but generally applied inconsistently by parties to a conflict as a way of justifying their own means and ends and delegitimising the means and ends of their stated enemy. The observation that the term is loaded is well made in the retort 'One man's terrorist is another man's freedom fighter'. However, this does not disabuse us of entitlement to use the term, but simply directs us to exercise due caution in its use.

A fair indication that an action is deserving of our condemnation as terroristic is that it is indiscriminate or disproportionate in either intent or effect or likely effect. Actions perpetrated outside the just war conventions of what may be permitted in waging war are likely to be terroristic. The killing of innocent civilians as a result of blanket bombing – without due discrimination or realistic chance of their escape – is terroristic. Because such actions have been perpetrated by a state does not mean that they cannot be terroristic. When I accepted the request of an Iraqi journalist to shadow my 2005 election campaign, I took the opportunity to ask her a few questions. Yes, the US-led bombings of Iraq had been horrific and she and her family did not know from one moment to the next whether they would be extinguished in a second, as their neighbours had been. Yes, Saddam's removal had simply replaced one set of problems with a new set of problems. Certainly, she had been terrorised by the US.

I have already described the perpetrators of the Twin

Tower attacks as terrorist; but that does not mean that violent countermeasures taken by states to combat them could not also be terrorist. The violent measures taken by Bush, and supported by Blair, with the stated intent of overcoming an 'axis of evil' were themselves generally evil and certainly terroristic. The anti-terror measures were not even claimed to be effective by key orchestrators, like Donald Rumsfeld, who repeatedly warned that the chances of future attacks on the US became more not less likely as the 'war on terror' proceeded.

It should come as no surprise that nobody has a monopoly on the administration of evil, although the Bush regime would have had us believe that the suicide bombers were somehow radically other than human. The concept of evil recruited by Bush (whether or not he realised it) was essentially a bipolar, Manichean one, that would have it that the stated enemy was intrinsically evil and that the US was intrinsically good.

But that is not a credible ideology. As Milgram's experiments of 1963 famously showed, unassuming citizens can be led to do cruel, inhumane things, if so directed. In the experiment, subjects were asked to administer an electric shock to a person behind a glass screen, unaware that the device was not real and the recipient was only pretending to be in discomfort or pain. However, most subjects continued to administer increasing voltages of shocks (so they thought), in spite of the actor's convincing cries of pain and appeals to stop. When subjects hesitated, the experimenter asked them to continue and most did for several more steps beyond that. What this shows is that people are either naturally inclined, or institutionally habituated, to comply with requests from people said to be in charge. The presumption of obedience to authority was abused to devastating effect by the Bush regime in Guantánamo and Abu Ghraib; the command-control structure of the armed forces required nothing less.

Guantánamo

The Green Party has campaigned dedicatedly for the release of Britons and others, held in Guantánamo Bay without charge, trial or any kind of due process. As the true scale and horror of what was going on there became apparent, Azmet Begg, the father of one of the detainees Moazzam, was heard speaking about the kidnap of his son in the middle of the night, the sudden loss of mobile phone communication, and the months (later years) of torment their family had to endure – first not knowing what had happened to him, or why; and then knowing what had happened to him, but not why.

At a meeting in the House of Commons in 2003, Mr Begg implored the US that if his son had done wrong, then he must be tried; if not, then he should be released. Somehow, whilst sharing the father's torment, I feared that he was conceding too much about a situation he knew he had limited, if any, control over. I could not but speak out against a part of what he said; 'It doesn't matter what he has done, he must be released!' My defiance was informed by the clear probability, in light of what we already knew had happened to his son and others, that he was innocent *of any wrongdoing*, and that there was no crime he could have committed which could have justified such intolerable and inhumane treatment of him already. Therefore, he should have been released unconditionally. In a letter written from the Camp, Moazzam Begg records the many abuses he personally experienced and witnessed, and his torment over the fate of the family he loved is that of any father: 'By what legal authority was property and money confiscated, leaving my wife and young children destitute and penniless, in their wake?' (Guantánamo, 12 July 2004)

When, years later, I spoke to a group of youngsters about the atrocities being perpetrated in Guantánamo still, *they were literally disbelieving*. As I explained again that, no, these prisoners were being held without charge or trial and subjected to degrading treatment,

I realised how unreal it did sound. Unfortunately, this is one of the battles we have faced, to report truth and have truth understood; incredulous though it might have sounded.

When the revelations of torture in Abu Ghraib came out in US soldiers' trophy holiday snaps – what was our reaction to pictures of Iraqi men suffering degrading, inhumane treatment? Did it make us angry at the US, and ashamed to be an American if we were American? No, actually it made me feel ashamed to be a *human being*.

The unconscionable actions of the Bush regime have resulted in intolerable pain and unbearable suffering for tens of thousands throughout the world. His actions were neither intelligent nor just. Greens speak out and fight against all injustice, regardless of who is the perpetrator. Might is not right.

Gaza carnage

The conflict in the Palestinian Occupied Territories has also arguably worsened since 9/11. The 'war on terror' rhetoric has served as an additional, stated pretext for aggressive military strikes against the Palestinian people by the state of Israel. One cannot but remain incredulous at the claim, for example, that Israel's 22-day bombing campaign of Gaza in December 2008 through to January 2009 was aimed at putative Hamas terrorists, not the civilian population at large. Israeli spokesperson Mark Ragev described the onslaught against the Gazans as 'worthwhile'. But the extent of disproportionality was evident to all: 1,300 Palestinians killed and 13 Israelis killed. None of those deaths was worthwhile, and each side sought to dispute who was responsible for aggravating hostilities. But the facts do speak for themselves.

Even on Israel's preferred version of reasons that led to their onslaught of Gaza, there can be no question that their use of force – with the inevitable innocent dead that would result – was indiscriminate, disproportionate and in clear violation of the laws of war. When, as each warring day unfolded, we learned of the hundreds upon hundreds of Palestinian children killed by Israeli rocket-fire, we could not but feel sickened by the merciless Israeli offensive. Any and all decent citizens and politicians felt justified outrage and revulsion at the carnage meted upon the children. Such means were neither morally permissible nor likely to result in conditions conducive to peace in the region. A British MP summed up the reaction of many who wrote to the papers at the time: 'Israel's attack on Gaza is not just wrong but madness.' (Barry Gardiner, 17 January 2009)

The injustice suffered by the Gazans was compounded by the refusal of the BBC to broadcast an appeal of the Disasters Emergency Commission in January 2009. The BBC gave as a reason that it would risk undermining public confidence in its impartiality. They were probably right about that, but certainly not for the reasons they supposed. By bringing the scale of human suffering into our living rooms, viewers would have rightly concluded that Israeli armed forces were directly responsible for grave human rights violations. They might also have inferred that the BBC had not properly interrogated what Israel was doing and had taken them too much for their word. In all this the Palestinian children continued to suffer and die.

The attempts by Israel to deceive the world about the rightness of its onslaught in Gaza did not go unchallenged then, and should be disposed of here. Firstly, when confronted by the disproportionate death count on the Palestinian side, the Israelis sought to blame those deaths upon the Hamas operatives who they say they intended to kill instead. Israel said that Hamas had used innocent Palestinians as 'human shields', and so had somehow brought those deaths upon themselves. But this fails to take account of the moral obligation not to kill the hostage. Therefore even on its preferred version of events – and any sensible explanation of causes – Israel still killed those Palestinians. It was Israel's finger on the trigger, not Hamas's.

Secondly, Israel would construe the Hamas rocket launches or suicide bombings upon its own population as somehow morally beyond comparison to its own, far more deadly use of violence. But this fails to take account of the fact that the destructive capability that Hamas has had at its disposal is as nothing compared to Israel. That is not to justify the use of violence by either side, or to recommend that Hamas should seek more destructive capability, far from it; it is simply to point out that, for whatever reason, a stated enemy may feel compelled to resort to using themselves as a weapon instead of having no weapon at all.

This imbalance in weapons on either side is described as a case of 'asymmetry' by theorists of war. But rather than representing an escalation of the means of waging war, the resort to suicide bombing is a sign of desperation. Cherie Blair and Jenny Tonge both caused controversy for being prepared to state the obvious truth that Palestinian suicide bombers must have been driven to desperate means because they felt they had nothing to lose – such was the extent of their systematic oppression and suffering. In a 2002 statement condemning terrorism in all its forms, the Green Party sought to recognise that, 'people experiencing a sense of injustice in the face of overwhelming and indiscriminate force, resulting in the deaths of innocent people, and who feel that their voice is not being heard, may feel that they have no other way of expressing themselves than by creating spectacular acts of violence.' (RPD02.4)

A British journalist reporting on the Middle East conflict once asked the telling question 'What makes a man [or woman] hate so much they are prepared to die in order to kill?' That is the extent of human misery and desperation to be found in many quarters of the Occupied Territories. To seek to *understand* the causes of conflict, hatred or unconscionable violence is *not to attempt to justify* such actions. It is an attempt to diagnose the problem in a way that could assist us in addressing some of the causes. That is why the International Court of Justice ruled in 2004 that the Israeli wall is contrary to international law; that it must be dismantled immediately; and that reparations must be made good to the Palestinian people.

The Green Party affirms that we cannot build a secure, lasting peace in the region without redoubling efforts from either side to resolve enmities by negotiation instead of violence. Whilst recognising the atrocities committed by either side, we cannot but envisage a path for peace without a reversal of the oppressive conditions that have been inflicted upon the Palestinians by Israel over six decades, and contrary to a series of UN resolutions.

In a review of its policy in 2009, the Green Party reaffirmed its commitment to pursuing justice for the Palestinian people as a precondition of progress: 'The Green Party calls on Israel to repeal its present "law of return" because it is incompatible with the full exercise of human rights and discriminates against Palestinians because they are not Jewish. This racial discrimination symbolises the unfairness of the present arrangements in Palestine, and will have to be addressed before any solution can be agreed.' (MfSS, IP624) It is unlikely that progress can be made without determined supervision by the international community, neighbouring states; and, in particular, the US, given its special relationship to Israel, both as a moral counsel and as an arms supplier.

State police

There is a fine line between *state police* and a *police state*. Former good; latter bad. The police have a duty to serve us all and a right to expect our cooperation in return, but they are not beyond the requirement to act justly in the process – and to be seen to be. Alas there has been a systematic erosion of civil liberties in the UK, due to the negative impact of badly framed or excessive anti-terror legislation and, in particular, the use of highly questionable policing tactics since 9/11 – such as the 'kettling' tactics used to 'control' the G20 protestors in 2009, and the police violence which led directly to the death of Ian Tomlinson. Greens seek to redress this imbalance by promoting a *service-led* culture within the police force, in which they are an integral, representative and visible part of the communities they would serve. This will help to counteract the sense that they are generally remote from us – somehow anonymous, or actually aggressive.

Policing can be an extremely challenging vocation, and with the right training also immeasurably rewarding. The funding of safer neighbourhood teams, fronted by police community support officers, will be prioritised, and the idea that this is not a proper policing role will be corrected by affording it the status in the profession it deserves. Policing on foot or by bicycle may not be seen to be as glamorous as hot pursuit by helicopter or turbo-powered vehicles, but, pound for pound, the benefits to society are greater. A *cultural shift* will not only lead to the citizenry being better served, due to the adoption of intelligence-led, community-based policing, but a correction in the public's exaggerated fear of crime out of due proportion to the probability of crime or terrorism actually occurring.

Tackling both crime and the causes of crime will be a priority for a Green government, in terms of better design of urban spaces; improved social and sports facilities for people of all ages and backgrounds to enjoy and share; and the resourcing, not abatement, of informal policing roles. Greens would increase 'resources for caretakers, attendants and staff on estates, railway stations, parks and other public areas' (MfSS, CJ116). Greens are also committed, where possible, to make greater use of *community sentences* instead of custodial ones. The focus of justice would be for the offender to make reparation to the community; not to face retributive infliction of harm for its own sake. Punishment will continue to play a role but less of a role. We take the current levels of men, women and youth imprisoned to be both unacceptably high and counterproductive because of the 'great cost to their future rehabilitation, as well as to their families, the taxpayer and society in general.' (CJ340) A socially just society is one in which the resentments which sometimes foster crime will not be allowed to fester.

CCTV

CCTV as an aid to crime prevention has got out of control. One can acknowledge that CCTV footage is sometimes useful, even critical, in securing a conviction in certain circumstances. But the more relevant question is whether it is generally a better way, pound for pound, of directing limited police resources. A 2007 report by the Royal Academy of Engineering entitled, 'Dilemmas of Privacy and Surveillance: challenges of technological change' concluded that it is 'far from clear that surveillance brings intended benefits' and that the harms often fall more upon those who are racially stereotyped. I would say that CCTV also contributes to an irrational sense of siege; or a sense that since a crime is being recorded then one need not intervene, even when it is relatively safe to do so. It were as though crimes were no longer real until or unless they got recorded and broadcast as part of a national campaign.

Call this the *Crimewatch UK CCTV syndrome* – the tendency to mediate, validate, and therefore distance oneself from the communities one belongs to through the closed circuit camera and the television set; but that is conducive to alienation, one of the causes of crime; not to social cohesion, something that would help abate the preconditions of crime.

Greens would promote a more diverse police force – in terms of both gender and ethnicity – to try to combat prejudice in the police, where it occurred, and to boost the confidence of the public in them, in turn. Official police studies demonstrate that people from ethnic minorities are at least four times more likely to be stopped than those classified as white. Yet the arrest rate resulting from such stops is both highly marginal and shows no significant difference per category. Therefore, if you are *innocent and black* you are more likely to face police detention than if you are *innocent and white.*

There is no place in society for the race-based policing tactics these statistics betray. The use of stop and search under Section 44 of the Terrorism Act 2000 or Section 60 of the stop and search (non-terrorist) powers would be limited to proper intelligence-led policing. This is to advance nothing less than the findings of a 2007 MPA report, entitled 'Counter-Terrorism: the London Debate', which accepted that Londoners were 'unhappy to accept the existence and use of a police power which requires no reasonable grounds other than its own authorisation,' and concluded that, if the police were unable to demonstrate the effect of the power in countering terrorism, then they should stop using it, in order to limit 'the damage done to community relations'. In 2009, the European Court ruled that the use of random stops and searches was unlawful. Instead of abiding by this ruling, the current government would seek to appeal against it.

Stockwell shooting

Unjust racial profiling played a part in the fatal shooting of Brazilian worker Mr de Menezes at Stockwell Underground by armed police in July 2005. The police compounded their error of using 'dark skinned' as a reason to initiate 'hot' pursuit of the suspect, by contradicting themselves on a form when later recording his colour as 'white European'. On the day, crucially, the Metropolitan Police adopted rules of engagement known as Kratos that would enable an officer to shoot to kill solely on the basis of a remote command.

There was fevered public reaction in the days and months following the killing, both out of sympathy with the deceased and his family and outrage that the police had made such a fatally dramatic mistake. Two official reports were compiled by the IPCC and trials were conducted by the coroner and under health and safety legislation. There is much information in the public domain but the right conclusions have yet to be drawn. What lessons should be learned?

Firstly, the rules of engagement that were subjected to considerable debate in the aftermath of the killing – provoking comment from both senior police officers and politicians – should have been put to the public before then, for some form of legislative scrutiny that enabled approval or rejection. Instead they were adopted in 2003, with minimal announcement, and only after input from Israel about their own use of the tactics. In addition, some of the rules were kept secret.

Second, comments made by the police after the shooting, demonstrated that they had not, in many cases, understood the preconditions for using their own lethal commands. Under Kratos, lethal force may only be used when 'absolutely necessary', and in strict compliancy with Article 2 of the European Convention of Human Rights. Instead, some police assumed that the concept of 'reasonable force' could be made to apply; but that is a far weaker condition.

Third, confusion about the *exceptional circumstances* under which the rules could be entertained and applied was exacerbated by incompetence on the part of the operational commander on the day. In the 2007 trial, Commander Cressida Dick maintained that when she gave the order to 'stop' the suspect, she did not mean to have him shot dead. However, the *Stockwell One* report takes issue with this: 'In the context of what had occurred it is clear that this was more than a normal police stop order and that in those circumstances she should have said that KRATOS had not been engaged and that CO19 [specialist firearms unit] should not shoot unless there was an absolute justification.' (*Stockwell One*, 20.47: 127). Whilst the prose is understated the implication is clear. Dick's failure to clarify what she meant, even if one took her word for it that she did not mean to have the suspect shot dead, was grossly incompetent and culpable. The rules had been explicitly engaged during the pre-shooting briefing and *Stockwell One* goes so far as to criticise the language used by one DCI on the day as inciting the firearms team: 'Well prepared, up for it, deadly and determined.' (IPCC November 2007, 18.92: 104)

Since the command 'stop', under Kratos, was being used as shorthand for shoot to *kill*, there can be little doubt that any failure to make explicit a contrary intention constituted negligence of a high order. The command could have reliably been known to bring about a fatality and did in fact. It should also be learned that the use of the term 'stop' is not explicit enough, under any circumstances, for the action it is supposed to sanction under Kratos – and not explicit enough to rule out that a commander might, as any kind of a defence, seek to subsequently claim that *she did not mean what she said*. Perhaps the use of the word 'KILL' could be substituted, to help focus the minds of the firearms team that they were indeed 'up for it'?

The Green Party for the London region drew up policy for the 2008 GLA elections, calling upon the Met to *abolish* the shoot-to-kill option under Kratos. Lethal force may remain an option outside Kratos, but only under the legal protections afforded by the European Convention of Human Rights. This position properly takes into consideration the need to minimise the risk of great harm – and injustice, with lethal results – done to innocent people, through possible false identification as suspects. Moreover, there is an inbuilt bias in the Kratos rules (as drafted) to shift the presumption of responsibility for exercising lethal force up the chain of command, from the firearms officer to a remote commander. But this risks seriously disempowering the shooter, in a time-critical scenario, from engaging with the suspect in ways that could have helped to establish their threat level or none.

Even if it is agreed that there can be circumstances in which it is permissible, or required, to shoot to kill a terrorist, in order to save a greater number of innocent bystanders, the Kratos rules are arguably ill-suited to perform that function in such a crowded environment as London – with its multiple opportunities for misidentification and miscommunication.

Nor can it be taken for granted that the public would consent to such a tactic being made available, even with further protections. So long as there remained a problem of misidentification – with the added injustice that some minorities were going to be at greater risk of groundless suspicion – it is arguable that, other things being equal, *it is far worse to be the victim of a police mistake or incompetence*, than to be the victim of a suicide bomber. Both harms are instances of being in the wrong place at the wrong time, but we should take ourselves to be in greater control over what tactics the police may take themselves to have resort to in the name of defending those they claim to serve.

Even if your average London citizen found themselves, in some sense, better protected by the police resort to a Kratos rule – and was at reduced risk of being misidentified on racial grounds – I have some faith in the assumption that they would not wish upon their innocent neighbours or commuters a greater risk of harm or injustice through the application of an ignorant racial profile that they happened to conform to. This is what is meant by standing *shoulder to shoulder*.

In 2008, after ten weeks of deliberation, the jury into the coroner's inquest into the de Menezes shooting returned an open verdict and concluded that his death was at least in part caused by six failings of the police – yet the coroner ruled out unlawful killing as a verdict open to the jury. In 2010, Commander Cressida Dick received an award in the New Year's Honours list. If the Green Party needed yet another reason to want to disestablish the monarchy, and the trappings which it facilitated, here it was.

The sheer *obscenity* of seeking to reward an individual whose culpable incompetence had been a major cause of the death of an innocent man beggars belief.

Fire!

We continue to damage the extraordinarily beautiful planet we live on. If politics is about means and ends, then green politics is about knowing how to live within our means, and to promote such means, so that others may have ends at all. A major theme of the book is the idea that there are purposeful values to be had in the world, both in the manner in which we live, and the social and environmental goods to which we may aim. A society organised along green political lines is a just and meaningful one. I set out to explain why today, more than ever, the advance of green politics offers our best hope for preserving the planet for future generations and repairing some of the damage for the sake of other living things.

Before drawing things to a close, let me summarise the main findings of the last chapter. Greens are committed to a just society in which the basic needs of food, housing and health, must be available for all, irrespective of how well off somebody is. A Green government would provide everybody with a guaranteed Citizen's Income – to which the rich would contribute the most on average – to enable people to pursue their vocational and creative interests in a balanced way; and without negatively impacting on people's ability to perform, or desire to learn, socially invaluable voluntary roles.

We looked at the value of a public service ethos worthy of the name and what Greens would do to reverse the mistakes of decades of ill-conceived privatisation initiatives. We would return the railways to public ownership and invest in transport infrastructure to prioritise human scale walking and cycling, followed by public transport; and remove the impulse for people to want to use carbon-intensive and environmentally polluting transport modes. We looked at how the introduction of marketing strategies by the Royal Mail – where previously there had been few or none – resulted in a deterioration of service. We diagnosed the customer-led, target-focused culture – as typified by the dysfunctional request of a company to catalogue a spontaneous expression of gratitude – as emblematic of a deterioration in public service delivery of health and housing needs. We affirmed the Green commitment to a properly funded national health service, free at the point of use, and outlined the policy of right to rent as an alternative to the right to buy policy that had left us with a housing crisis.

We stressed the importance, for Greens, of a state-funded, high-quality, comprehensive school education, and the philosophy of lifelong learning as a means of promoting learning for its own sake. We criticised the government's instrumentalist attitude to higher education as frustrating even their own stated plans to assist workers to retrain – by penalising those who already had qualifications in different subjects to the ones they wanted to learn. We saw why Greens found it necessary, in order to foster social inclusion at an early age, to encourage a critically aware approach to religious education in schools; and to end state funding of faith schools, and to ensure that their admissions criteria are overseen by local authorities. We looked at how trenchant religious ideology could result in social exclusion and unjust outcomes.

We critically evaluated the harms which would befall various sections of society – in particular gays – if a religious ideologue was taken at his word. We explained how anti-discrimination initiatives were bolstered within a human rights framework that Greens would articulate and defend.

In the section entitled, 'Free speech and dirty hands' we looked at the confusion that could result from a misconstrual of the notion of free speech as an absolute right. We instead outlined a libertarian account of speech that accepted boundaries for good reasons, such as protecting against the undue risk of harm to minorities. We looked at the difficulty of managing platforms with extremist speakers, such as the BBC's inclusion of the BNP.

In 'War and Deception', I focused on the Green Party's moral and political reaction to the warring actions of the US and UK in Iraq, within the framework of a just war tradition and its preconditions of going to war and waging war. We saw how the pretext for Blair's insistence for going to war had no moral or evidential basis; and instead resulted in unconscionable harm, devastation and death to ordinary people innocent of wrongdoing. We exposed the plagiarised and doctored UK dossier on Iraq's WMD for the fraudulent and dishonest enterprise that it was and questioned whether it wasn't more appropriate to indict the warmongers in the international courts than to risk shaking their hands.

In 'State Terror', I outlined the Greens' moral and political opposition to the outrages of Guantánamo Bay, Abu Ghraib, and the assault on Gaza; taking pains to refine our definition of terrorism in a way that would help us to see clearly actions for what they were and to overcome state-sponsored propaganda and double standards.

In 'State Police', we saw how the Greens would pursue service-led, intelligence-based community policing to combat crime and the causes of crime, instead of over-reliance on CCTV and other alienating strategies. We reviewed the fatal shooting of Mr de Menezes in the hands of an over-zealous armed response unit and their incompetent commander – in the context of the risky use of a shoot-to-kill rule of engagement that was neither understood by the police nor enjoyed public consent. Greens would abolish those rules.

War footing

The lesson of Chapter 3 is the recognition that we must move, and in some cases return, towards a more public-spirited society – locally and globally. Only when we have better internalised and practised the communitarian and humanitarian ideals that social life has to offer, will we stand a fighting chance of overcoming the climate change emergency. James Lovelock has characterised the group solidarity that is required of us at this point in human history as the need to get on a 'war footing'. I would have to disagree with those who find such nomenclature offputting – and it should now be clear to the reader why I would describe this as a self-pitying response that illegitimately deflects attention away from the external problem. The usage is justified given how close our analogy is to the public spirit and group solidarity that was engendered and directed during the Second World War. The analogy is strong on a number of grounds: we face a man-made threat; we can best overcome it by acting as one, e.g. by rationing; and we have an emergency.

Counteracting false hierarchy is a necessary part of getting us to think and act more intelligently. We need to think global and act local. We are not thinking global enough. We have seen how people, as in the past, have been got to do the most unconscionable things through a command-control structure; with little, if any, avenue for dissent or overhaul of bad decisions. An egalitarian society is an empowered one, in which people are closer to the decisions which affect them, and less inclined to shield themselves from the difficult questions that would need to be answered by everybody acting collectively, and which could not be addressed by a few conscientious sorts, even if they were in charge.

The war effort against man-made climate change could start with a dismantling of the military-industrial complex to a more appropriate level. In the contexts of chapters on Workers Rights and Peace and Defence, Greens say, 'We encourage the creation and implementation of plans for the conversion of targeted military and other industries, into socially useful and environmentally friendly production. These conversion strategies are best produced at a local level with the involvement of the workers; the local community; consumer groups; Green businesses and financial institutions, and other interested parties (e.g. environmental experts).' (WR632) The war footing analogy gives us a powerful new context for calling people to this particular action, in addition.

Beauty and truth

Radical politics, Climate Change mitigation and a Just Society are what makes the Green Party a force for good and deserving of the voter's serious consideration. We saw, in chapter one, why Greens understood that gaining political office was not an end in itself but a vital means towards delivering radical political, social and ecological solutions fit for the scale and urgency of the challenges faced by humanity today. The Green Party thus heralds its optimism in a democratic politics worthy of the name. We recognise a human responsibility to both non-human animals and future generations, in pursuit of long-term, selfless values. By choosing to appeal to voters, and to respect them, as rational agents, we seek to engender trust in politics. Greens are responding to a calling, not making a career move.

In the chapter on Climate Change, we saw how overconsumption both contributed to environmental degradation and ended up leaving consumers far less happy than they would have liked – contrary to the assertions of aggressive advertising. Greens would seek redress through a massive programme of investment in renewable energy and energy efficiency, with the twin goal of reskilling workers in sustainable industries.

Inspired by recent films, we addressed reasonable doubts about our ability to overcome the climate change challenge, affirming that human beings could be motivated through cooperation and altruism in the service of non-selfish goals. We looked at the role of contraction and convergence as the means to advance global mitigation further and faster than is currently the case. We examined the case of the employee who took environmental exception to being made to deliver a Blackberry device to his boss, and won a court ruling against unfair dismissal on the grounds that his beliefs were worthy of serious, credible and cogent assent. I sought to reinforce the transformative experiences of the first astronauts through the imaginative device of Postlewaithe's archivist.

I asked an existential question on behalf of the human race, What futile hope was it to have our archive posthumously read by an extraterrestrial being compared to the hope that we could determine our own destinies? This latter hope is at least within our sphere of influence. A chance encounter with an alien is not.

I predict that future leaders and wannabe heroes will promise us technological change that would enable us to have our cake and eat it. Instead of moving to slash our collective greenhouse gas emissions at a stroke, by moving towards a vegetarian diet – redirecting livestock feed towards starving masses and abating cruel farming practices, at the same time – wannabe heroes will seek to despoil the planet with GM seeds and agrofuels. Instead of biting the bullet of global overpopulation by making contraceptives more readily available – in conjunction with sex education, and by promoting female empowerment and fighting poverty around the world – wannabe heroes will seek to put those least able to afford the impact of climate change to work in clothing factories.

Technological change may offer us some hope; but probably little more than the building of an archive station that will survive a battering from extreme weather. We didn't progress beyond the stone age because the stones ran out; but we will have to progress beyond the consumerist age because the oil runs dry. We could come to our senses before that, of course, for reasons that this book has sought to convey: *the true answer lies within ourselves.*

Coming to our senses, however, does not mean leaving the blockbuster movie *Avatar* feeling as though life is not worth living. Yet according to web forums, fans of the film have contemplated suicide thinking that if they did it, they would be 'rebirthed in a world similar to Pandora where everything is the same as in *Avatar*'. A forum moderator has described the film as 'so beautiful, it showed something we don't have here on Earth', and a psychiatrist has posited 'visual realism' as the reason for people to want to escape permanently into the film.

There is no question that the human creativity and past technological invention that gave audiences the freedom to watch films and critique their reactions (even if they would only pity themselves), is *more beautiful* than what can be depicted in the film itself – as a precondition of the film's creation. It is sad that the fans do not realise this – yet.

Perhaps there is a reasonable context for the man who shouts 'FIRE!' in the auditorium, after all? Not only would he be literally warning people that the planet is burning, but he would be helping them to shift their *frame of reference* away from the comfort of the cinema to the planetary emergency outside.

But we have nowhere to evacuate.

Life is short. Perhaps many of the ideas contained in this book have a shelf life beyond the next general election.

Why vote Green? Because true politics requires nothing less.

Archive

Entries marked † are referred to in the text.

Newsprint

Shahrar Ali, 'The BBC, impartiality and the Gaza appeal', letter, *Guardian*, 27 January 2009

† Shahrar Ali, 'Questions surrounding Bush visit', letter, *Evening Standard*, 19 November 2003

Martin Bentham, 'Home Secretary bans Islamists behind Wootton Bassett march', *Evening Standard*, 12 January 2010

Tara Brady, 'Admission policy at Jewish school was "race discrimination"', *Harrow Observer*, 31 December 2009

Nicholas Cecil, 'BBC has given the BNP leader a massive boost, says Le Pen', *Evening Standard*, 23 October 2009

Vikram Dodd and Michael White, 'Shooting to kill needs no warning', *Guardian*, 27 July 2005

† Barry Gardiner, 'Israel's attack on Gaza', letter, *Harrow Observer*, 15 January 2009

Susanne Goldberg, 'Secret footage of teenager's pleas exposes life in Guanatanamo prison', *Guardian*, 18 July 2008

John Harris, 'How 30 years of right to buy has changed housing for ever', *Guardian*, 30 September 2008

Philip Hensher, 'The BBC is too impartial to suffering', *Independent*, 26 January 2009

Amelia Hill, 'Working lives "intolerable" for millions in the UK', *Observer*, 4 May 2008

Afua Hirsch, 'G20 death: 44 seconds of video that raise serious questions for police', *Guardian*, 8 April 2009

Sandra Laville, 'Courtroom clashes as family questioned hearing's fairness', *Guardian*, 13 December 2008

Paul Lewis, '"All hell broke loose": Oxford graduate held at gunpoint by police', *Guardian*, 19 July 2008

Caroline Lucas, 'The growing population', letter, *Guardian*, 16 July 2007

Mark Lynas, 'Six steps to hell', *Guardian*, 23 April 2007

† Karen McVeigh, "'I'm a green martyr" – judge rules activist's beliefs on climate change akin to religion', *Guardian*, 4 November 2009

George Monbiot, 'Paying for our sins', *Guardian*, 18 October 2008

† Mark Prigg and Jonathan Prynn, 'Experts fear decade of the gadget is over', *Evening Standard*, 13 January 2010

Susanna Rustin, 'My first election', *Guardian*, 21 December 2009

Avi Shlaim, 'How Israel brought Gaza to the brink of humanitarian catastrophe', *Guardian*, 7 January 2009

† Jo Steele, 'Are you feeling blue?: Why the utopian world of blockbuster movie *Avatar* is leaving fans depressed', *Metro*, 13 January 2010

†'Troops told "shoot to kill" in New Orleans', ABC News Online, 2 September 2005

John Vidal, 'Global warming is killing 300,000 a year, says study', *Guardian*, 30 May 2009

† David Ward, 'Whistleblower to face tribunal', *Guardian*, 10 October 2003

Books & reports

† ACPO, Manual of Guidance on Police Use of Firearms, www.acpo.police.uk

Ali, S., 'Everyday Risk and the Deliberate Release of Genetically Modified Crops', in Almond, B. & Parker, M. (eds), *Ethical Issues and the New Genetics: Are Genes Us?*, Ashgate 2003

Ali, S. 'Is There a Justifiable Shoot to Kill Policy?', in Brecher, B., Devenney, M. & Winter, A. (eds), *Interrogating Terror*, Routledge 2010

† Al-Marashi, I., 'Iraq's Security and Intelligence Network: A Guide and Analysis', *Middle East Review of International Affairs*, vol. 6, no. 3 (September 2002)

Begg, M., *Enemy Combatant: A British Muslim's journey to Guantánamo and Back*, Pocket Books 2007

Berry, S., *Mend It!*, Kyle Cathie 2009

† BMA manifesto, *Standing Up for Doctors, Standing Up for Health*, BMA 2010

Collier, J. L., *The Rise of Selfishness in America*, Oxford University Press 1991

Dobson, A., *Citizenship and the Environment*, Oxford University Press 2003

Faber, M., *Under the Skin*, Canongate 2000

Fevre, R., *The Demoralization of Western Culture: Social Theory and the Dilemmas of Modern Living*, Continuum 2000

Gaita, R., *Good and Evil: An Absolute Conception*, Macmillan 1991

Glover, J., *Humanity: A Moral History of the Twentieth Century*, Pimlico 2001

† Green New Deal Report 2008, www.neweconomics.org/publications/green-new-deal

† Helm, D. & Hepburn, C. (eds), *The Economics and Politics of Climate Change*, Oxford University Press 2009

† IPCC, *Stockwell Two* (August 2007). www.ipcc.gov.uk/index/resources

† IPCC, *Stockwell One* (November 2007). www.ipcc.gov.uk/index/resources

† Iraq: Its Infrastructure of Concealment, Deception and Intimidation, number10.gov.uk

Lever, A., 'Why Racial Profiling Is Hard to Justify', *Philosophy and Public Affairs*, vol. 33 (2005): 94–110.

London Green Party, *Change London for Good*, 2008 London manifesto

† London Green Party, *A Quality Life, for a Quality London,* 2004 London manifesto

Lord, C., *A Citizens' Income: a Foundation for a Sustainable World*, Carpenter 2003

Lovelock, J., *Gaia: A New Look at Life on Earth*, Oxford University Press 2000

Lucas, C. & Woodin, M., *Green Alternatives to Globalisation: A Manifesto*, Pluto Press 2004

† Milgram, S., *Obedience to Authority: An Experimental View*, Tavistock Press 1974

† Mill, J. S., *Utilitarianism, Liberty and Representative Government*, Everyman 1936

† MPA, Counter-Terrorism: the London Debate (2007), www.mpa.gov.uk

Norman, R., *Ethics, Killing and War*, Cambridge University Press 1995

Orwell, G., 'Politics and the English Language' (1946), in Jackall, R. (ed.), *Propaganda*, Macmillan 1995, 423–37.

Owen, D., *The Hubris Syndrome: Bush, Blair and the Intoxication of Power*, Politico's 2007

† Palmer, M., *Moral Problems: A Coursebook for Schools and Colleges*, Lutterworth Press 2005 (Lincoln example)

† Reynolds, M., Blackmore, C. & Smith, J. (eds), *The Environmental Responsibility Reader*, Oxford University Press 2009

Rowlands, M., *The Philosopher and the Wolf: Lessons from the Wild on Love, Death and Happiness*, Granta 2008

Sartre, J-P., *Colonialism and Neocolonialism*, Routledge 2001

Singer, P., *Writings on an Ethical Life*, HarperCollins 2001

Spowers, R., *Rising Tides: The History and Future of the Environmental Movement*, Canongate 2004

Stephenson, J., *Letting Go of the Glitz: The True Story of One Woman's Struggle to Live the Simple Life in Chelsea*, Crown House 2009

Thompson, S., *Countering the Crisis*, Green Left 2009
Wall, D., *Babylon and Beyond: The Economics of Anti-capitalist, Anti-globalist and Radical Green Movements*, Pluto 2005

Web resources

http://another-green-world.blogspot.com
http://greenladywell.blogspot.com
http://greenmpforvauxhall.blogspot.com
http://jimjay.blogspot.com
http://theonlygreenroom.blogspot.com
www.brixtonpound.org
www.carolinelucas.com
www.carolinelucasmep.org.uk
www.darrenforlewisham.org.uk
www.greenparty.org.uk
www.greenpartyni.org
† James Balog's Extreme Ice Survey presentation. www.ted.com/talks/james_balog_time_lapse_proof_of_extreme_ice_loss.html
www.jeanlambertmep.org.uk
www.london.gov.uk/assembly/members/johnsond.jsp
www.london.gov.uk/assembly/members/jonesj.jsp
† Moazzam Begg's Letter from Guantánamo, 12 July 2004.
http://news.bbc.co.uk/nol/shared/bsp/hi/pdfs/01_10_04.pdf
www.norwichgreenparty.org
www.petertatchell.net
www.policy.greenparty.org.uk (Manifesto for a Sustainable Society)
www.scottishgreens.org.uk
www.shahrarali.net

Film

† *The Age of Stupid*, dir. Franny Armstrong, 2009
† *An Inconvenient Truth*, dir. Davis Guggenheim, 2006
† *Avatar*, dir. James Cameron, 2009
† *Pitch Black*, dir. David Twohy, 2000

About the author

Shahrar Ali first trained as a biochemical engineer before studying philosophy. He has a PhD from UCL on the topic of lying and deception and teaches philosophy for lifelong learners. He joined the Green Party in 2002 after working in the European Parliament. He was lead author of the Green Party's 2008 London manifesto and regularly speaks for them in the media. He is the Green parliamentary candidate for Brent Central in 2010.

There is only one political party in the UK committed to a fair, sustainable, standard of living for everyone...

" The success of a society cannot be measured by narrow economic indicators, but should take account of factors affecting the quality of life for all people: personal freedom, social equity, health, happiness and human fulfilment. "

Green Party Manifesto for a Sustainable Society

You can be a part of it
Join online today
www.greenparty.org.uk/join